Garden Musings

Essays on gardening and life from the Kansas Flint Hills

Garden Musings

Essays on gardening and life from the Kansas Flint Hills

JAMES K. ROUSH

iUniverse, Inc.
New York   Bloomington

Garden Musings
Essays on gardening and life from the Kansas Flint Hills

iUniverse books may be ordered through booksellers or by contacting:

iUniverse
1663 Liberty Drive
Bloomington, IN 47403
www.iuniverse.com
1-800-Authors (1-800-288-4677)

ISBN: 978-1-4401-3785-3 (sc)
ISBN: 978-1-4401-3787-7 (dj)
ISBN: 978-1-4401-3786-0 (ebook)

Printed in the United States of America

iUniverse rev. date: 4/8/2009

Contents

Preface to the First Edition

A bit presumptuous to write a preface "to the first edition", isn't it? Well, sorry, this is in fact the first edition, and any implied suggestion that this will ever be popular enough to require a second edition is solely in the mind of the reader.

What follows is an entirely personal collection of essays on gardening and life, meant solely to relieve this gardener's daily frustrations and lamentations over gardening in general and particularly gardening in Kansas. It is not a blog because I'm a bibliophile, not a hacker, and it's printed rather than placed on the internet so that I don't get criticizing emails from the less polite readers (or internet fruitcakes). It is written to celebrate life and living as a middle-aged married male, if such a diminished creature can be considered as having a life. I believe that it contains some kernel of value to novice and experienced gardeners alike, wherever you may be. I recommend, however, reading it in the dead of winter when you will not otherwise be wasting the precious hours of sunshine in your own gardens.

The essays are in pretty much random order and can therefore be read or skipped in any order. Kansas gardeners may be particularly interested in essays on the Kansas gardening conditions, but the rest of the world may empathize better with my thoughts on lawns or my rant on the Home and Garden Television Network. If you're a start-at-the-beginning type, then you may be disappointed in the fact that there's not an ending, but feel free to revisit a favorite essay if you don't feel satisfied at the end. What the heck, most importantly, please start wherever you will be enticed to continue reading.

For convention and to try to keep the reader's interest, I have used the common name of plants, followed most times at first use with the scientific name italicized and in parentheses (but not "quoted and away from everything else in the middle of the other side"). Those who don't want to be burdened with the scientific name will find this useful as you can possibly train yourself to skip past the parentheses and not be bothered with the Latin. I have made all attempts within my power to be sure that plants are identified by the correct scientific name and are correctly spelled. To be sure, different sources sometimes spell names differently and botanists (and microbiologists) make a living changing the scientific names on organisms to confuse the rest of us, thus providing us with that ever-sought opportunity for "life-long learning." Therefore, if mistakes are present, the fault is entirely due to those who create plant labels, since I copied the names off the plant labels when I bought them. Likewise, for convention, I have referred to printed sources or television episodes by the respective author and then the italicized title of the work. I also appreciate a good index to a gardening book, even one full of simple essays, so I have prepared one that I hope will easily let you find whatever crap I had to say about your favorite plant so that you can disagree with me once again.

Above all, happy reading, and happy gardening. And if you didn't get the reference to "quoted and away from everything else in the middle of the other side," then you weren't raised in the 1970's and you desperately need to look up the lyrics to Alice's Restaurant, an old Arlo Guthrie tune.

I Garden (In Kansas): Therefore I Suffer

Henry Mitchell, in *The Essential Earthman* said "Wherever humans garden magnificently, there are magnificent heartbreaks. It is not nice to garden anywhere. Everywhere there are violent winds, startling once-per-five-centuries floods, unprecedented droughts, record-setting freezes, abusive and blasting heats never known before." I believe Henry was attempting to lighten the misery of those who think they have gardening tribulations by proposing that all gardeners share the weather and environment as a burden. Likewise, Christopher Lloyd, the great English Gardener, in *In My Garden*, tries to tell us that we should not expect gardening to be easy, saying "Gardening is not for enjoyment....There is no virtue in enjoyment."

In the best tradition of Mr. Mitchell, who appears in his essays to be a bit of a curmudgeon himself, and in deference to Mr. Lloyd, I say "Humbug" to both of ya. While I appreciate Henry's attempt to lighten my worry load, I really think he underappreciated the difficulties of gardening in Kansas because all the problems he listed and more are seen here in plots as small as one acre or less. Oh, I'd heard the sayings attributed to old Kansas pioneers like "In God We Trusted, In Kansas We Busted." And the jokes; "Hear the one about the Kansas farmer who prayed for rain? Not for himself, but so his seven-year-old could see moisture fall from the sky?" But the evidence keeps racking up that I, the Hoosier-born offspring of several generations of farmers, chose through ignorance to garden in a delightful area combining the world's worst soil and an exasperating climate, all augmented by various man-made and natural catastrophes such as tornadoes, droughts, prairie fires, hail, drenching rains, ice-storms, late freezes, boiling summers, and seventy mile per hour winds. Henry, you have no idea of pain.

I came to Kansas at the end of a ten year drought in this area and my father, who drove down in the moving van with me, will fully admit that on seeing the still-brown Flint Hills in June, he wondered what the hell I'd got myself into. He still brings it up approximately every time he visits, yet in the twenty years we've lived here the droughts have since stayed away or at least have been short enough to be seen as minor natural variation on annual rainfall. A year after we moved here it had greened up. Three summers later we had record floods in this area in June, floods sufficient to flood the "five-hundred year flood plain." Floods sufficient that people were vacationing from Nebraska to view the waterfalls across the reservoir spillway (it seems that it takes little to excite Nebraskans; a tree here, a little rain there and they're piling in cars for the sightseeing novelty). In twenty years, I've seen the effects of a solid month of >100°F weather and no rain in my garden. I've seen the effects of two solid weeks of -20°F and no rain. I've seen the effects of ten inches of rain in a week in a clay basin that normally only gets thirty inches in an entire year. I've seen the effects of seventy mph straight line winds, prairie fires, and locust plagues. Honestly, Henry, have you heard of the Dust Bowl? Here's a quiz, where was the Dust Bowl? Was it in New England? California? Washington DC where you lived and gardened, Henry? No, it was in Kansas and the surrounding states. In the widespread droughts of the 1930's, only one spot in the US became famous for farms buried by dust. Right here, from Texas through Kansas and into Nebraska. Try reading Timothy Egan's recently published *The Worst Hard Times* for a real idea of what the Dust Bowl really was.

It was, however, the local Extension Master Gardeners course that brought the horror that is Kansas gardening home to me. Dr. Alan Stevens of the Kansas Extension Service runs a large and popular commercial test garden in Olathe. It's one of those gardens where commercial breeders and growers from all over the world submit their best new varieties for assessment of their hardiness, flowering potential, and other attributes. In point of fact, those breeders and growers from all over the world fight to have a place in the Olathe test garden. In one of our EMG classes Dr. Stevens stated it simply; "Everyone wants their plants grown here in our test garden because if they survive here and do well, they'll survive anywhere in the world." And he wasn't kidding either.

Not all parts of gardening in the Flint Hills are completely bad however. I would have said that the constant undulation of the hills gives us good drainage for all plants that are able to cling to the average thirty degree slopes of the hillsides, despite the clay and rocks which impede the flow of groundwater. When we've had particularly good rains, my plants, particularly my rose garden, sit in what amount to clay swimming pools for weeks. On the positive side, only four days elapses before the wind and sun dry the soil into bricks so the plants don't usually have time to drown and the clay holds enough moisture in summer that they take a while to wilt. Rose roots don't need oxygen, right? On the particular day as I began this essay, we had 3.5 inches of rain overnight and the city of Greensburg, Kansas was wiped off the map yesterday along with nine souls dead and a misfortunate multitude of injured citizens. Yet today, a day later, the outside wind is howling from the north, feeding a storm to our south that will bring us yet more chances for tornadic fury, and the rain is coming down sufficiently hard that I can see the normally dry "draws" to the east and west of the house have become rivers. My pond and that of my neighbor are overflowing their dams and eroding soil in their drainage paths. My south garden beds sit in a small lake formed on the immediate terrace of my backyard and my vegetable garden has enough erosion that I can foresee, millions of years hence, the New Grand Canyon that has begun right here. Yet my basement, opening onto the ground level below, remains dry and if I ever feel the need to start learning the exact dimensions of a "cubit", I can rest complacent that by then the rest of Kansas and the US east of the Rockies will be only a memory at the bottom of a new Mesozoic inland sea while I'm building my ark of solid clay on this hillside.

Landscapes in Day-Glo Orange and Purple.

There are many perplexing questions to life on this earth. Never mind questions like "why does God do bad things to good gardeners?" The obvious answer to that question is that S*** often just happens. Far and away, the most difficult question of existence to me is that of where on this earth do most landscape designers get their training? And do these programs actually train these individuals that the best and most maintenance-free landscapes are those formed of purple japanese barberry, 'Stella de Oro' daylilies, spireas, and yellow-tipped junipers? Or do the designers just fall back on these plants because "it's what everybody else is doing?" Is there some mysterious part of psychologic makeup that leans those persons with a tendency to like flaming oranges and muddled purples to take up landscape design courses at esteemed universities?

Of all the most hideous combinations one could devise, it is the combinations of the aforementioned plants that seem to be the mainstay of our local landscaping here and by my meager travels, everywhere else in the Continental United States. During drives around my town, whole houses and additions are seen bounded and bonded by puke purple blobs, accented by day-glo orange flowers, and punctuated by the faintly musty hues of most flowering spireas. Just today, I drove by new landscaping near some apartments in town that consisted of thirty-eight purple barberries in a massive bunch on a berm with three gold-tipped junipers at the ends and apex of the planting. One wonders why the designer didn't just paint the ground mauve, edge it in highway orange and let it go at that. The most expensive homes in town, I noticed today, are increasingly landscaped in alternating Juniper-Purple Barberry-Juniper. In other areas, the barberries are the background for numbers of 'Stella de Oro' again and again and again. And if it isn't Stella, they serve as backgrounds for Rudbeckia 'Goldstrum', yet another flower of the same jarring orange hue. Sometimes, as in front of my workplace, lime-green spireas are the foreground for the ubiquitous barberries. I recently saw what I believe is the ultimate in poor taste, an entire house surrounded exclusively by alternating yellow and burgundy barberries. Not only is the color choice hideous, it doesn't even have the diversity of different plant or leaf form to recommend it. I'm convinced it's all a mass conspiracy driven by those who are of Communist or Socialist leaning and perhaps aided by those who believe that modern art and taste requires defacing religious or patriotic symbols.

Now what, you should ask, do I have against junipers, barberries, and Stella's? Other than the incredibly grating combination of murky purple and screaming orange-yellow? I suppose there must be some people that think this combination as the height of tasteful coordination. After all, there were also those in the '70's who thought leisure suits and wide white trouser belts were the hit of fashion. It unfortunately sets my teeth on edge to think about any of these as a tasteful expression although under threat of torture, I'll admit to owning a leisure suit in light blue back in the '70's as might many of my male readers. But let's take the plants and their combinations one at a time and forget about our past indiscretions, shall we?

Spireas first. I have a grand total of none in my garden, and could only be induced to be near them if they were planted on my newly dug grave and I couldn't claw my way free in a lateral or heavenly direction. I find spireas among the most boring shrubs in existence and their boorishness is only compounded by their muttled, unclear colors. Muted pinks, dirty whites, or pale lilac-blues are the height of spirea splash. The only thing glaring about the colors in spireas are the mad pink or purple types such as spirea 'Anthony Waterer', which, of course, seem to be the most popular types in general use. Cut them to the ground every year, they grow back, on stiff stems, their foliage unappealing, and their flowers too airy to be eyecatching. And clearly, searching deep in my psyche, the thing I don't like about spireas most is the simple fact that they are too similar in flower form to the tall weeds that necessitated I spend my boyhood on the seat of a tractor and bushhog. Those were Common Ironweed (*Vernonia fasiculata*), wild purple ones that grew tall and hard on the Indiana prairie. With me it is a visceral reaction. One look at spireas and I want them cut down and out of my sight. I see none of the pest-be-damned attitude of these plants, none of their drought-tolerance, none of the cheery "always in flower" nature that in any other plant I would covet. Actually I prefer the purple wild ironweed in the garden to most of the named varieties of spireas; at least the color of ironweed is a good clear royal purple.

I actually like barberries especially when used as specimen plants and I am particularly fond of the new varieties like *Barberry thunderosa* 'Rosy Glow' and some of the lime-green varieties, but there is nothing really low maintenance about them. Unless one is willing to see how big they get, they need a yearly trimming which involves multiple punctures to the human trimmer during cleanup and leaves them looking both bare and mottled as the deeper foliage is green and only changes slowly back to purple. Some have proposed barberry as a deer-resistant plant and I can only say that it simply shows that the deer have better tastes than the owners of the yards they dart through. I do have a 'Rosy Glow' which highlights the northeast corner of the house as a specimen plant that I never trim, water, or look at, and I have two 'Gold Nugget' dwarf barberries which provide a nice yellow-green accent to a perennial bed.

Junipers? Nothing wrong with junipers except that there are only two types used widely around town, whether purchased for their weight in gold from the local nurseries or bought for $5.95 at the SuperWalmart. Most of these remain unfailingly green year-round, except at the tips which turn yellow, the color of which is lost each time the juniper is pruned, and except for the areas which become loaded with bagworms. I have a number of junipers and likely will gain more since according to many gardening authorities one of the more advanced stages of gardening sophistication is the development of an evergreen garden. I've been mentally toying with designing a bed of the latter, but haven't yet had the pocketbook or hauteur to begin. In the meantime, I have a low edge bed of *Juniperus horizontalis* 'Blue Rug' which nicely keeps the weeds suppressed in an otherwise useless area and sitting in the middle of that a *Juniperus procumbens* 'Greenmound' whose bright green color coexists nicely with the blue-green of the 'Blue Rug'. At the southeast corner of our back patio is a grouping consisting of a dwarf spruce, *Picea glauca* 'Conica' in front of which is a *Juniperus chinensis* 'Old Gold' and flanking that on either side two *Juniperus horizontalis* 'Youngstown Andorra', which are darker green than the 'Old Gold' during the summer and turn plum-purple in the fall and winter. My only other junipers currently are a pair of *Juniperus horizontalis* 'Mother Lode' which I've moved a number of times and have yet to let settle down, with the consequence that they are barely visible at present and ready to succumb to the summer heat.

Lastly, the marvelous Stella. 'Stella de Oro' was a once-in-a-lifetime advance in daylily breeding, a daylily that would bloom from spring to fall and stayed a nicely contained clump instead of spreading wild over Wyoming. One wonders though, if God was simply playing one of his little tricks and decided to make the first long-season daylily a day-glo orange that would nauseate 95% of the population. Or is the color of Stella merely a byproduct of the fact that it was released in 1975 and thus fit right in with the avocado greens and harvest golds popular in the 1970's? Why not a nicer, more blendable yellow such as that now available in 'Happy Returns'? I see Stella being used everywhere, and everywhere is just too much orange, particularly when paired with burgundy barberry. In fairness, I recognize that not everyone is quite so color-attuned, or ahem, sensitive. My father, for one, loves his many clumps of Stella's (placed everywhere around home, of course, by a professional landscape designer). It is also true that I once had a visitor at our garage sale comment on the beauty of a clump of Stella's arranged around my mailbox (I'm sorry, I didn't know any better at the time) and proclaim how lucky my wife was to have a husband who grew such flowers. I immediately got a shovel and offered her half the clump, both to rid me of it and to cast further shadow on the woman's poor unfortunate husband.

If I'm simply more than abnormally sensitive to these ubiquitous landscapes, it's because of my first and only experience of working with a real honest-to-god landscape designer/landscaper in our area. In purchasing a new ranch-style home in a brand-new addition, complete with sub-topsoil clay as the primary surface around the house, we began our odyssey into suburban landscaping by feeling we should have, and might be able to afford, the front and back yard landscaped by a professional. In my defense, I'll point out here that at the time I had not yet been bitten by the gardening bug and I did not have the slightest idea at the time what any given plant was on sight. Having heard all the propaganda on how a professionally landscaped home would enhance the resale value, and knowing nothing about how to proceed ourselves, we requested, and obtained a free design plan from the most longstanding and recommended nursery in our area. An individual came out, measured the yard, and was most impressive for an hour or so sketching ideas and walking around in a visionary fashion. A week or so later, there followed a surreal sit-down session where the landscaper pointed to the various circles on an impeccably-prepared design plan and pulled out associated plant pictures saying "for this area, I'd recommend the GoldCrest Juniper", introducing each plant as if it were royalty and daring me to challenge that it was the best, nay the only, plant worthy of considering in that spot. Suffice it to say, we now had a great plan which consisted almost exclusively of gold-tipped junipers, green junipers, barberries, and spireas in front of the house in a rather large terraced bed that took up about 70% of the front lawn space. There was, separate from the beds, a single Redbud tree to accent the south corner and "frame" the house. The overall size seemed excessive to me, but in the landscaper's defense, he was merely going by the "depth equal to three times the height of the house" rule for dimensions as expressed in all good landscaping manuals. The cost also seemed excessive, with the final estimate approaching one-fifth the value of our new house.

Based on cost, we immediately asked for the front bed to be decreased to about one-third of the designed size and completely ruled out any professional landscaping of the back yard. As an aside, the latter turned out to be the first good decision I'd made since later plantings in the back yard gave me immense pleasure and education during my early attempts at gardening. With a second design plan, we then gave the go ahead for the planting of approximately nine junipers of three types, six spirea, and a trio of barberries, all of which was accomplished along with the terracing at a price I now know to be approximately 5X what it would have cost to do it myself, including labor.

I perceived this weekend that Man is a hopeless experiment and we are doomed for early extinction. The local downtown flower arranging store, an establishment of previous taste with a forest green front and tasteful white lettering on the windows, has been repainted. The store front is now fuchsia, with pink edging. It is only missing a few Stella daylilies in the window to be indistinguishable from the landscape around it.

Statue Searches

Picking an appropriate garden statue is one of the most important and lasting decisions a gardener makes in the garden. First and foremost, the proper statue must fit within one's sense of the place, or, put another way, it must go along with the "feel" of the garden. It must be of an appropriate and lasting material, one neither affected by weather nor eroded by bird droppings. It must be of subdued color so it does not clash with its surroundings. It must, in Kansas, be partially composed of dense stone or lead lest it tip over in the slightest breeze. For many gardeners, it must cost less than gardener's primary house. Thus, the proper choice presents a dilemma for even the most accepting and liberal of gardening personalities. I've been frustrated recently in my search for a decent statue for the garden. To make my own issue worse, friends would be the first to tell you that I'm not generally known as either liberal or accepting. I've been searching for quite a long time now, but cost, design, and size have not intersected in my favor at present.

It goes without saying that the proper statue for my garden must be formed of concrete. Carved marble is a bit beyond my pocketbook (although I'd be happy to be proven wrong), and carved wooden statues don't seem very prevalent outside of Alaska or the Pacific Islands. Even carved granite will likely be a bit too costly, let alone the difficulties of moving it into my garden. I detest even the slightest consideration of any statue made of the polymers available everywhere, thus seeming to be the current fashion, particularly in stores such as Pier One and Hobby Lobby. In the first place, they're much too light for Kansas winds and would likely disappear from the garden on the first night, only to be found a week later in a cornfield near Springfield, Missouri. In the second place, what impulse seizes the creators of these plastic monstrosities that they're not content with just using a material unfit for natural surroundings, they also feel that the things should be painted suitable more for placement in the local carnival than in the garden? I mean, really, even the statues other than the gnomes look like they've been decorated by twelve-year old girls who were just pulled away from trying out Mom's makeup for the first time. I'm just looking for plain, simple concrete. It doesn't even have to be a dyed concrete, grey is fine, particularly since I've noticed that many of the colored concrete statues sold locally end up fading or flaking away to the gray beneath.

A primary obstacle in my search is the lack of availability of what I view as appropriately-sized statues. I believe that it's time to add a statue to my garden that is viewable at eye level, something taller than the abundantly available turtles or rabbits that every garden store seems to stock. Trust me, I've searched far and wide. To my chagrin, there is not a single commercial nursery within two hundred miles of my home that carries a statue over thirty-six inches in height. In other words, the statues available to the vast majority of Kansans are acceptable for viewing only if one is either a "height-challenged" individual or if one plans to walk around the garden in a permanent stoop at the waist. Yes, there are pedestals, but trust me, putting a twenty-four inch statue on a twenty-four inch pedestal just leaves a too-short and too-thin statue on a too-short pedestal for the scale of my rose beds. Do local stores really believe that most of the population wants to wander around the garden looking at plants and structures placed at knee level? The local nurseries and horticultural centers carry lots of small rabbits (of which I already have a collection), turtles, gnomes, curled up cats and dogs in repose, stepping stones, and other similar ground-level structures. Many carry small St Fiacre or Virgin Mary, or Christ statues, but only in the sizes suitable for worship by Hobbits. And what of the gargoyles? Does anyone else find it strange that most garden stores carry a plethora of varying gargoyles? Are they really selling that well to the public and what does that say about American gardeners? And if they sell so well, why is it that I've never seen them in someone else's garden?

I confess that I currently have a very nice statue of a studious young lady reading a book, a birthday gift from my wife and daughter that I like very much, but the whole thing, including the pedestal, stands thirty-eight inches tall. It is suitable for the cozy informal area where it's placed, but it would be dwarfed if it was the focus of or was visible only in the greater garden. I also, as mentioned previously, have a collection of concrete rabbits in various poses (probably the reason my garden attracts wild rabbits by the dozen), but one expects rabbits to be small. And I have a medium-sized Easter Island head on a pedestal facing due East, as it should, and my good taste here has already been confirmed as noted elsewhere (see my essay titled *The Home and Garden Network*). What I lack, nay, what I crave, is a decent life-sized classic garden statue.

In the 630 miles down I-70 between my boyhood home and current home, there is not a single statuary retail establishment, but there is one which happens to exist about ten miles south of my former home and I visited there recently in hopes of finally finding a suitably sized statue. And there were several to choose from, but here arises the second problem with locating an appropriate statue; the design. In about two acres of large concrete statues, there were none that I felt appropriate to place in my garden. Now, let us be clear. Setting aside the life-size concrete buffalo, the painted Indian, the race car, the giraffe and the elephant, the statues of little boys peeing, and the forty-five different large gargoyles available, there were in fact several statues that I considered. I should state here that what I'm generally looking for is a classic statue in feminine form. I'm not asking for much, a Venus de Milo or similar arty form is what I envision for a certain site in my rose garden. It can be partially nude, perhaps even with an accidentally undraped and blurred breast, but must otherwise be tasteful. The Indiana statuary didn't have any Venus's, but did display a statue of Eve presumably as formed in the garden of Eden (she held an apple in her hand although it was some time before I noticed the apple). My wife and daughter thought her the best statue in the lot and encouraged me to take her home. However, this particular life-sized Eve had full breasts which I can only describe here as "pert." I'm sure I've seen those same breasts on the pages of Playboy Magazine, back in my younger days when I looked at such things, and they looked no more natural on the statue than they did in the magazine. To make it worse, when viewed from behind, her buttocks were as fully formed as the Michangelo's David replica standing beside her. I'm afraid I draw the line at having a statue in my garden that will be physically arousing when first viewed every morning. It's just too exhausting to have around. And as a general rule, if it can't pass the Supreme Court's definition of pornography, it probably isn't suitable in any garden outside of California or the Playboy Mansion.

There was another statue in the lot that perhaps would have worked in a Kansas garden. Titled "the Flower Girl", it resembled a maiden perhaps of Germanic origin, fully clothed in a smock and bonnet, carrying a flower basket. One could easily have seen it as a young pioneer girl, suitable for the Flint Hills, and again, my wife and daughter were all for carrying home this statue. But she was a little too "plain" for me. The statue had what I can only describe as a thick waist and flabby arms. Thus, these two statues, the only ones available in the size and cost I wanted, left me with the age-old male dilemma; the choice between the girl nobody wants to dance with or the one you can't take home to your mother. I left without a statue. My search went on.

In Omaha Nebraska, on a business trip, I finally found and brought home what I believe is the perfect statue for my garden. Titled "Aga Marsala", whatever or whoever that is, it is a five foot chaste, dressed female, hair braided and up on her head, cleavage visible but covered, standing and holding a book while engaged in reading. In that matter, it fit everything I needed; arty yet not obscene, and it matched my smaller existing statue of the seated angel reading, thus giving me a garden theme; the reading garden.

Garden Of My Dreams

My garden in the Flint Hills of Kansas is the garden of my dreams. Our French cottage-style brick house sits on a ridge with a view of the scenic tallgrass prairie north, south, east, and west. The house front faces almost due north and the front landscaping is an enormous perennial garden bed. The garden continues around on both sides to the terraced hillside in back, a southern exposure. Stately oak, elm, pecan and cottonwood trees surround the back garden and provide a serene milieu within which lay the more formal garden and paths. An eight foot tall red brick wall, with a coppiced top that looks like the wall surrounding the "lower garden" at Mount Vernon surrounds my garden inside the trees and protects the tender plantings from the searing winds of Kansas. Just within the wall, a semi-circle of fully grown lilacs provide a green background to soften the brick on the west, and espaliered apple and pear trees against the wall soften the eastern and southern wall. A sculpted iron gate leads out of the garden and to the utility area (compost pile and storage) to the due south, but from within the garden the gates on the south and southeast offer quick glimpses at the rolling grasslands beyond it. Within the lilac and fruit tree backdrop sit a number of irregular but complimentary-shaped beds that are mixed shrub and perennial beds all edged in white limestone.

Each bed is covered in six inches of good shredded bark mulch and the earth beneath is dark, moist and loamy prairie soil laying over five feet deep in many areas. The beds are separated by six foot wide red-brick paving stone pathways laid in herringbone pattern and all contain layered plant heights and foliage colors to enhance the viewer's interest. I have named the beds for the predominant plant that I started each bed with; thus there is the peony bed, the hydrangea bed, the viburnum bed, the east rose bed, the shrub rose bed, two mixed iris and daylily beds (the "old" and "new"), and the evergreen bed. Lest one picture each bed as a boring collection of cultivars within a single genus, however, the names are really just for my convenience and don't indicate a lack of horticultural diversity or imagination on my part. For example, the bed I call the hydrangea bed does contain five hydrangeas at the ends and along it (*Hydrangea microphylla* 'Pink Diamond', *Hydrangea paniculata* 'Limelight' and 'Bulk', *Hydrangea quercifolia sp*, and *Hydrangea quercifolia* 'Little Honey", but it also contains a bright red crape myrtle (*Lagerstroemia indica* 'Centennial Spirit') six roses, a snowball viburnum (*Viburnum opulus* 'Roseum') , a buddleia, ten daylilies, eight irises, two hollyhocks, two Rose of Sharon (*Hibiscus syriacus* 'Notwoodtwo' and 'Rubis'), eight ornamental grasses, a Sweet Autumn clematis (*Clematis paniculata*) and twenty various other perennials and shrubs. As one of my great passions is roses, I'll detail the roses in this bed; the red Rugosa 'Linda Campbell' and pink shrub roses 'Bonica' and 'Martin Frobisher', Hybrid Teas 'Taboo', 'Chuckles', and 'Country Dancer', 'Dr. Brownell', 'Crimson Glory', the Canadian rose 'Champlaign' and, of course, the grandest of grandifloras 'Queen Elizabeth'.

The more immediate surrounds of the house are landscaped not in the classic American foundation pattern of evergreen, barberry and spirea, but are raised perennial and shrub beds of sufficient size to compliment the two story brick house. The immediate front of the house is softened by a number of Oriental Hollies including the variegated 'Honey Maid' (*Ilex merserveae*), along with a boxwood

(*Buxus microphylla* 'Green Mountain'), viburnum (*Viburnum fragrans* 'Mohawk'), blue clematis (*Clematis* 'Romona'), and honeysuckle (*Lonicera* 'Florida Red'). In front of those are mixed beds of perennials including phlox, shasta daisies, Knifopia, yuccas, *Knautia macedonia*, daylilies, roses, Weigela, peonies, sedums, grasses, lilacs, and ornamental strawberries. The retaining walls of the house beds are also brick to bring the house further into the garden and they slope to follow the contours of the land, and the walkways to the door and garage are brick pavers with moss growing between the pavers. To the west of the house is a bed of forsythia and lilacs, placed along the garage pad for early spring bloom and to provide much needed color and fragrance in an area seen daily as we come and go. To the east, a hillside of purple-leaved honeysuckle (*Lonicera japonica* 'Purpurea') controls erosion above and along a line of deciduous trees, and the more immediate house foundation bed holds a red-flowering peach (*Prunus persica* 'Rubroplena') to soften the corner, and a yellow-twig dogwood (*Cornus stolonifiera*) in the foreground.

Alas, the garden I just described exists only in my dreams and perhaps in the far future, even though I can see it as clearly as I can see the computer screen this is being written on. It is true that I live in a brick house on a ridge with a good view of the Flint Hills, and that the main garden beds are primarily to the south of the house, but many of the details of the preceding paragraph have yet to be realized. The stately trees currently are on average five foot high and the formal brick wall surrounding the garden exists only in my imagination along with the knowledge that I someday need to enclose the garden to help it fit the place and help the plants to survive (the prairie wind is definitely not a figment of my imagination). I'm also aware that I'll have to win the lottery in 2020 to actually pay for construction of the wall, so in the meantime, I've determined that I will enclose the garden with a hedge of upright ornamental grass, perhaps with *Miscanthus sinensis* cultivars 'Northwind' or 'Gracillimus'. A few of the lilacs that were mentioned are growing at present, bare-rooted specimens planted two years prior, but the espaliered trees, which I have seen impeccably maintained at Mount Vernon, are sadly missing here both due to time for growth and due to my laziness to trim and train them. The forenamed beds exist, but the shrubs within are still quite small because my extreme parsimonious nature is perfectly offset by my patience to let small plants grow. The beds are edged with white limestone, but for reasons of necessity and security. The limestone edging is to keep the roving prairie fires out of the bed mulch. "Fires?" you ask? Ah, that's another subject for a later rant.

The paths between beds are grass, not herring-bone brick, and mowed natural prairie grass rather than perfectly maintained bluegrass carpet at that. The mulch of the beds is not six inches thick, but it does average two inches at much expense and back-breaking labor. Last year I added over two hundred bags of mulch to the various beds and this year I added over one hundred bags to the beds immediately surrounding the house and used hay, straw, and leaves to mulch the lower beds. In my stingy defense, however, the mulch is sufficient to keep most of the weeds in controllable numbers, and it does preserve the moisture and temperature of the soil nicely and do all those other delightful mulchy things. The soil of the beds, it goes without saying, is native, unamended Kansas clay, the initial double-digging of which I chose to forego as it would have required a backhoe and a crew of seven muscular laborers. Actually, that's not entirely correct. The soil over most of my garden expanse is composed of approximately six to twelve inches of decent rich prairie soil, beneath which lays a more or less continuous six to twelve inch thick layer of flint chips of varying sizes and shapes, and below that is a seemingly unending layer of solid, anaerobic, yellow-red clay extending to wherever bedrock may be (more on that later as well).

The most accurate descriptions in my fantasy above are the plants themselves, most of which existed and many of which still survive at present (okay, I'll admit that the 'Honey Maid' hollies bit the dust this year), and all of which I'm very proud of in terms of selection and placement. There's no backdrop except for the prairie hills, but for a mixed bed of shrubs, perennials, and rock, it is generally pleasing to the senses for most seasons and manages to provide some interest and needed aromatherapy to the passerby. In the spirit of Ken Druse's subsets of gardeners in *The Collector's Garden*, there is no doubt that I tend to be a collector of various plant cultivars rather than a gardener of the Jekyll artist's palette following. I rarely plant more than one individual cultivar or species in the same place, let alone groups of three or five as recommended by the gardening authorities, however, I have in several places gathered a number of peony cultivars in one spot, or daylilies, or iris cultivars together. As a gardener, I am focused on the beauty of the individual flower and plant, and less on the flow of form and texture, although I would like the overall result to be harmonious and any color of foliage or bloom to be distributed throughout the seasons.

Of Garden Writers and Reading

I confess that I, probably like many others, enjoy reading about gardening as much or more than I enjoy gardening. After all, when reading about gardening one can do so in a controlled climate, without the irritation of gnats or the delay of rain. In fact, rain itself can promote reading about gardening. Or one can choose to recline within the garden itself when reading, spread out on a hammock of one's choosing as the scents and breeze waft around. I don't have such a hammock yet, but I intend to build a gazebo soon and place a perfect hammock within it, far enough from the house that I can pretend to ignore calls, and surrounded by the garden.

I like reading varying gardening essays more than dry tomes about this certain aspect of gardening in gravel or that specific genus of plants. Essays about why we garden, essays about special plants, essays about tools, and essays about gardening people are what I enjoy most. There are in fact, many enjoyable whole books written about garden people. Those in the twentieth century were primarily written as biographies (although served up with occasionally spicy gossip as in those stories about Vita Sackville-West and the crowd she ran with). In the twenty-first century they seem to be written about groups of gardeners rather than single individuals, and these groups are consistently portrayed initially as curious and eccentric, although the writers seem to eventually conclude that their subjects are normal obsessive compulsive gardeners. I've recently finished Aurelia C. Scott's *Otherwise Normal People*, Amy Stewart's *Flower Confidential*, and Susan Warren's *Backyard Giants*. All are very good, entertaining reads, particularly the first of those which is about those rosarians who concentrate on showing roses, and the last of that group that covers the small group of obsessed gardeners who grow pumpkins and other vegetables primarily to make it into the record books.

I have found a few authors or garden writings that I enjoy enough to read over and over. The first group of authors is represented by a coven of writers who are full of acerbic remarks or dry humor about their gardens or other gardeners. Works by Henry Mitchell and Beverley Nichols come to mind here. Both these gentlemen write with a wry eye towards the foibles of humanity and the animal kingdom as regards a garden. Even on a second or third reading, one picks up different thoughts and sees new light as we develop as gardeners between readings. Christopher Lloyd also qualifies here, in his books such as *In My Garden*, but his English humor is so dry I sometimes miss the most enjoyable references. A second group of garden writers that I enjoy is one whose essays are thought-provoking or ground-breaking in terms of approach to gardening. Examples would be Lauren Springer Ogden's *The Undaunted Garden*, Sara Stein's *Noah's Garden*, and Michael Pollan's *Second Nature*. All of these works, and some others, are worth reading over and over for their unique lessons about gardening. And I read a third group of garden writers for the pure enjoyment of their writing and company as I read. Lustful Cassandra Danz would be one of those writers, as would Helen Dillon or Sydney Eddison.

I also have strong feelings about the format of gardening books that I read. Far too many books have been published which are written in order by the calendar year, and with chapters divided into January, February, and so on through December. How gauche. I don't need to see it in sequence to place myself in winter when we are talking about the blooming species of witch hazels, or in summer as we discuss how daylilies have been bred in every shade from orange to, well, orange. And probably, at heart, I don't like picking up a book with the story starting in the dead of winter and ending there as the gardening season winds down. Even worse though, are those authors who start in the middle of the gardening year, which leaves us feeling ungrounded and uneasy, seasonally out of sorts.

A note to the publishers and writers of the Time-Life and Sunset Garden series and other similar basic gardening tomes: I detest articles that seem to be copied over and over from one periodical to the next. I've seen the same articles published years apart in different journals (you know who you are). I also loathe simple how-to or reference type gardening books (unless we're considering *Hortus III* or *Botanica*) and no longer buy them. I resent that they seem to be proliferating on the garden shelves of major bookstores at the expense of more interesting and engaging reading material. Please, the world has enough books for beginning gardeners that tell us how deep and wide to dig a hole for a tree and how to make a compost pile. How many books can we read on "making an organic garden" or "easy lawn maintenance" or "success with perennials?" I expect most of these are contracted works where a publisher is sitting around thinking of things that might find an audience and then approach a well-known gardener to write one about beginning gardening (hypothesizing falsely that the beginning gardener would be more likely to be searching out a book to learn than an experienced gardener would). An exception to the group of advice on beginning to garden is Cheryl Merser's *A Starter Garden*, which is a decent read for a beginning gardener. Ms. Merser covers it all; tools, goals, walls, shrubs, roses, herbs, borders, and designs.

In the fictional *Death of a Garden Pest*, a garden mystery by Ann Ripley, she quotes one of the characters as saying "Some people get their jollies reading dirty literature; others get theirs reading rose catalogues." That just about says it all.

Rose Snob

Without the tiniest doubt, roses are the dominant shrub in my landscaping and form the beginning and the end of my gardening endeavors. I'm in love with the rose, and have been from the moment there was a piece of ground to call my own. We bought a house, I planted a rose, and a spark of passion was born. It was cardinal red hybrid tea 'Mirandy' I believe, that I planted first up against the house, although another old apricot hybrid tea, 'Brandy' soon followed, breaking up the formal landscaping design drawn up by the first and last paid landscape designer I'll ever use (see the chapter titled *Landscapes in Day-Glo Orange and Purple*). Shortly after that came my epiphany in the form of Thomas Christopher's *In Search of Lost Roses*.

I came across *In Search of Lost Roses* during a Florida vacation with my wife and parents, shortly after its publication, and somewhere, in Christopher's tales of rose rustling and pioneer women, in the accounts of the California ghost towns and the enduring graveyard roses, the spark blew into a flame. I learned, first from Christopher, of the differences between Old Garden and Modern roses. I learned of the connection between the rose and history, not just related to pioneer women taking 'Harison's Yellow' across the prairies, but history from the Romans forward tied to the rose. Many times during my life, as my passions shifted from one subject to the next, it was the history of the new subject that intrigued me first. So it was with Old Garden Roses. I learned how Old Garden roses were survivors, tough enough to survive droughts and neglect, impervious to fungus and wind, more cold tolerant, more scented, more voluptuous than Modern roses. I learned, in essence, to be a Rose snob.

The onset of the Internet revolution occurred fortuitously just in time to feed my rose snobbery. Using the newfound connections of the entire world, I was able to locate any number of Old Garden Roses and purchase them with the magic of plastic credit. I was quickly adrift in the sea of rose classes, jumping from the scented roses of the Isle of Bourbon to the centrifolias in the paintings of Dutch Masters and then marching with the Romans as they carried the Gallicas throughout Europe. Not just any modern, hideously overcolored, stiff-stemmed thorny excuse for a rose did I lust after, it was the historical roses that I craved. I learned to disdain the grafted rose in favor of roses grown "own root", described as a more natural and less diseased choice. I saw to detest the stiff, thorny, weak-constituted Hybrid Teas and their tendency to be annuals in a zone 5 climate. I read of the advances in rose hardiness and disease resistance of the modern shrub roses and of the older garden roses. In a year, my garden had added the mottled purple and white Bourbon 'Variegata de Bologna', the white damask rose 'Madame Hardy', the pink alba 'Great Maiden's Blush', and the incomparable mad gallica 'Charles de Mills'. Being naturally lazy and having no interest in spending my fall days covering roses, I had also branched into modern hardy hybrids such as the Ag Canada series of roses. And I had stepped into the footsteps of the pioneers, growing the yellow 'Harison's Yellow', although purchased from a mail-order nursery in my case instead of being carried in my trousseau on a wagon. To these, I added several roses "rustled" from local historic cemeteries and then rooted by me in my first successful propagation attempts. I keep two of those roses to this day, one a white semi-double of great fragrance but no known identity, the other a recruit from an 1850's circa grave in the Beecher Bible and Rifle Colony Graveyard a few miles east. That second rose is undoubtedly Konigan von Danemark, a soft pink Alba raised in Germany in 1826. What she was doing on the American Prairies twenty-five years after her birth and in the company of a group supported by fanatical free-stater Reverend Henry Ward Beecher, I'll never know, but in a very shaded family plot I noticed a single sickly cane of a pink rose and propagated it in the nick of time as the original rose only survived a few more years of dense shade before it joined the dearly departed beneath its roots.

Michael Pollan, in his classic gardening text *Second Nature* has a chapter on rose culture that perfectly fits my sentiments regarding fair rose. Pollan describes being introduced to "old-fashioned" roses by their display in the Wayside Gardens catalog. Ascribing human characteristics to the chaste 'Madame Hardy,' the enticing 'Maiden's Blush', and the over-endowed blooms of the modern Hybrid Tea 'Dolly Parton', Michael discusses the effects of human society on the breeding and selection of roses, concluding that it is impossible to separate the nature of the rose from human culture. Stating that he believed old roses would not be able to live up to what he had read, he then describes his first sight bloom of the damask rose 'Madame Hardy' as "beautiful," "aristocratic," and "poised." "Roots?" he asks for Madame Hardy, "What roots?" making the point that the blooms of this rose are of an otherworldly beauty that don't seem to be connected to this earth.

Madame Hardy is my most favorite rose. Some gardeners, when asked which plant is the one plant that they could never part with, would have trouble choosing between their favorites. For me, the choice has always been Madame Hardy. She was one of the first old garden roses I sought out when my own fanatic zeal for rose culture started. And she is indeed beautiful. And perfect. And…regal. So unlike the modern Hybrid Tea bush, Madame Hardy is a shrub with a perfect vase form, never suckering, never sprawling, and never coarse. Bred in Empress Josephine's court by her rose gardener, Monsieur Hardy in 1832, she was named for the wife of the breeder and she carries her obviously royal bloodlines in full view of the gardener. It doesn't matter that she blooms only once a year. It doesn't matter that her canes are often slender and her prickles are sharp. It matters only that every bloom is perfect. Image a white disk of flower petals laid flat, a green pip in the center, and just a touch of blush to the white disk as if the flower is embarrassed to be so beautiful and so bold at the same time. This is not the ever-covered form of the hybrid tea, reluctant to show it's innards in true Victorian fashion. Madame Hardy is definitely a French rose, blatant but delicate with its allure, spread wide for the world to see. And the fragrance! An unmistakeable, unparalleled, unique and strong scent of lemon and rose. I make sure I indulge in the first bloom every season as soon as it opens and I watch carefully for the last bloom of the season as well.

If you doubt that Madame Hardy represents rose perfection, I submit that this rose, herself, knows of her excellence and has taken steps to maintain her pedestal. Madame Hardy sets no hips and cannot be used to cross-pollinate other roses. She is a dead end in rose breeding. She allows no half-breed offspring to challenge her throne or steal away her lovers. Our Pop culture constantly discusses and debates the beauty of human women. I once heard a movie makeup artist who was asked who was the most beautiful actress she had ever worked on and the woman replied that it was Kim Basinger. The French have given us Catherine Deneuve as the perfect woman. And just this week, Clint Eastwood was quoted as saying that Angelina Jolie was undoubtedly the most beautiful woman in the world. Well, in the rose world, Madame Hardy is unquestionably the most beautiful. She is Josephine, Deneuve, Basinger, and Angelina Jolie rolled into one.

Sweet (Corn) Pain

I am simply unable to grow sweet corn to harvest in the Flint Hills. Do you have any idea how embarrassing it is for someone born and raised in Indiana to admit that they're unable to grow a crop of sweet corn? I never ever remember a failure of a corn crop in my father's garden, let alone in the field corn my grandfather cropped for life and money. But fail here, I do. Do you see the damning dilemma in which I'm placed? Can one ever call oneself a gardener without being able to provide a mouthful of homegrown corn?

Oh, I've tried. I've tried again and again. I've tried heirlooms (Golden Bantam and Country Gentlemen) and older hybrids and new extra-sweet varieties. I've even tried multicolored Aztec corn reasoning that even stone-age cultures could succeed with that. I've failed with them all.

I've concluded there is only one real insurmountable obstacle to growing sweet corn. It's because I garden in Kansas. No, really. I'd like to blame myself for the failures, and certainly in the early years that was a likely factor, but now I believe that the weather and insects simply take turns to deliberately and sadistically thwart my best efforts.

I began to plant sweet corn almost as soon as we bought the land (which others might describe less charitably as a hilly stone outcropping) we currently live on. A former student brought over a small tractor and we turned over the prairie sod and broke it up for a garden rectangle sixty by thirty feet. That first May I threw seed into the ground as I was accustomed to doing the entire time I was growing up in Indiana and waited patiently for the seedlings to break surface. And waited. And waited. In frustration, I redug up a portion of a row. No corn seeds to be found. I replanted. And waited. And waited. And got a few nice seedlings among a great crop of wild sunflowers. I weeded. I watered. I noticed the deer beginning to congregate around the electric fence prior to sampling the ripeness of the corn. I ended up with approximately six total ears, each of which had developed about 10% of the normal kernels, 90% of which were covered with corn earworm excrement. Most of the sweet corn we had to eat that year were delivered from Indiana by my parents and were perfect ears grown with no more care or watering than that given to the adjacent field corn on the home farm.

The next year I hit the books before planting. I surmised my error was in the timing of my planting. Sweet corn, it seems, needs a warm soil to germinate freely, in the neighborhood of 65-70°F. I purchased a soil thermometer as recommended by numerous gardening authorities (who probably receive kickbacks on each thermometer sold) and monitored the temperature of my garden soil hourly. At the exact recommended temperature I planted a number of rows and a mere ten days later noted a nice crop of seedlings sprouted and reaching for the sun. Success! Three days later however not a seedling was in sight, undoubtedly due to some nocturnal creature of evil. I replanted. June came without rain and no corn came up. The sweet corn we ate that year was delivered again from Indiana by my parents. Then and for years after, my parents would show up with the trunk of the car filled with several fifty gallon garbage bags full of so much perfect corn that we practically oozed the stuff from our pores for weeks after their visits.

This pattern went on with minor variations for a number of years as I researched my failures and attempted annually to gain a few ears of perfection. I read that I should plant in clumps of at least four rows to help wind pollination and I did. I learned that I was probably planting too deep in my Kansas clay, although I never remember worrying about planting too deep in the sandy soils of my boyhood. I learned that if I planted seeds in wet clay, they would rot despite the pink fungicide coating. I learned that if I planted and didn't water or get rain the germination would result in some corn in the row being seedlings while others were tasseling and forming ears. I learned that if I planted too late, the searing air temperatures of a Kansas July would keep pollination from occurring. I learned that there are approximately three good days in Kansas in June where corn that was planted in soil warm enough to germinate can successfully pollinate before the weather gets too hot. And I learned that no known commercial or historic variety matures in that window. Luckily my failures were always followed by the rescue corn delivered by my parents (charter members of the Red Kernel, a group devoted to rescuing gardeners from natural disasters).

I fought my nemesis, the wind, which threatened to blow over each stalk as soon as it appeared. Sometimes the entire patch merely looked like it was listing to starboard. Sometimes it looked like it had been driven over with one of the big highway rollers used to pack down asphalt. I fought the droughts, nearly doubling the monthly water bill for several months in the summer. I prayed for cool nights during early July so the corn could pollinate. I fought the rabbits and deer to a stalemate with electric fences, sonic blasts, and firearms.

But no matter how close I come, it is the corn earworm that mocks my research and trial efforts to beat it. I can now grow corn that grows tall if somewhat slanted. I can grow corn that approximately every other year will be filled out to recognizable rows of kernels rather than the occasional random kernel, and it will make it to harvest past the drought and warm—blooded critters. But when the corn I harvest is shucked, invariably approximately 50% of the distal ear is destroyed by one or more earworms that are blissfully resting among the kernel remnants and their own feces. I'm convinced there is no more slothful or disgusting creature on earth than a corn earworm, whose sole purpose and pleasure of existence seems to revolve around the need to convert sweet corn into feces and wallow in it. Other gardeners in this area tell me they have no trouble growing corn and that the earworms attack their corn as well, but that the ends can be cut off. Yes, the bad parts can be cut off the ears and the remnants still eaten if you can forget what the corn looked like covered in earworm feces. My children believe that ears of corn naturally grow to a length of only two inches and terminate abruptly at the end. But I cannot bring myself to eat it after I harvest it if it's had earworms. I've tried everything from dowsing the ears weekly in a variety of chemicals to individually placing drops of mineral oil on the silks of each ear. I've broken more pesticide regulations than an insane crop duster dumping a load of DDT on downtown Philadelphia. My next step is either to try a continual gentle mist of malathion, or to douse the ears with radioactive waste. I'm a native-born Hoosier, therefore I must grow corn.

And When I Thought It Couldn't Get Worse: "The Freeze"

Sydney Eddison, in *Fine Gardening*, June, 2008, stated "I pride myself in being a gardener of least resistance, believing the road to gardening success is best navigated by bowing to the fickle nature of weather." Up to a point in my recent past, I agreed with and tried to adhere to that philosophy, and had some success. But then the spring of 2007 and the following winter here in North-central Kansas brought me to my knees as it did most area gardeners.

The spring of 2007 here was such an enormous unprecedented disaster in terms of gardening that I will forever remember it as the year without flowers. It started with such promise because we had a beautiful warm March (in like a lamb, right?). The winter suddenly left in the second week of March to give us three blissful weeks of 70-80°F degree weather, lots of rain, and minimal wind. It was spring, and even the plants didn't know any better. The daffodils bloomed and receded, tulips began to open, lilacs made plans for attracting bees, the roses all leafed completely out, and the apricots, peaches and then cherries bloomed. Monday (April 2nd) it was 81°F at 3 PM. Then the forecast showed trouble coming, predicting a fast drop in temperatures to extreme lows. On Tuesday night it was 30°F. Wednesday, I covered the new, young roses and newer tender perennials. Covering plants to protect from cold is something not generally recommended by the gardening gurus in this area and is almost always futile, but I cannot help myself. I can't just stand by and watch the babies shiver in the cold. I always spend the days of late March and early April repeatedly covering and then uncovering small and struggling plants with empty buckets, plant containers from last year, and an occasional blanket. On Thursday, April 5th, came rain and snow during the day. The allowed me to obtain some wonderful pictures not only of daffodils in the snow, which I've seen here before, but lilacs, flowering almonds, quinces, and tulips, all bejeweled by the snow and ice. The book jacket cover is one of my lilac's covered by the snow during The Freeze. I'm being facetious about the pictures, of course. They appear wonderful indeed, but the thrill of the beauty of snow on lilacs is muted by fact that I know the blossoms and leaf tissue were dying as surely as my perennial spring sunburns peel. To see the pictures today is for me to also remember what the lilacs looked like three days later; shriveled and drooping leaves and brown blossoms. Friday, Saturday, and Sunday the weathermen noted all-time record lows for each day. My outside thermometer over Friday, Saturday and Sunday showed 19°, 17°, and 23°F respectively at approximately 7:00 AM each day. It was a time ever thereafter referred to by gardeners in this region as "The Freeze." It was bad. It was very bad. It was completely, undeservedly, unethically, unmercifully, unconscionably bad. It was the seven plagues of Egypt and the wrath of a vengeful God bad. Got the picture? Okay, I know that the median last frost date in my area of Kansas is April 15th, and I've learned not to chance tomatoes outside in this area before May 1st, but snow on April 5th and a very very hard freeze on April 8th is simply ridiculous. The Earth may be warming, but Kansas seems not to be.

In the midst of despair, the only positive note visible was that many of the really native Kansas trees, for instance the Cottonwood (the state tree), and the oaks and ashes, walnuts and pecans, all those trees seem to expect the worst of the weather and hadn't yet leafed out. But trees from other climates, like the buckeye, were green and damaged. I spent that entire first year after The Freeze wondering how many roses

31

I lost. It turned out that most of anything that wasn't bred at the Ag Experiment Stations in Canada was killed to the ground, including some Rugosa's. Many roses grew back from the roots since I grow a lot of own-root roses, but it'll be a couple of years before they reach any size again. I covered a few chosen roses on the nights of the worst lows, but I couldn't tell the difference between what I covered and didn't. All were wilted the next day and many dead to the ground by the next week. About 50% eventually leafed back out to some degree from the canes, but there were no buds, no flowers from the once-blooming or early season roses.

Irises and daylilies were all laid low and rotting on the ground, and not just for me on the prairie, but all over town. Woe to me, I listened to and took the advice of the KSU Extension Service and didn't do anything to clean them up. The result in most cases was a sagging mess that infected and rotted the tubers as well, killing the irises. I eventually lost over forty of seventy iris varieties. Well, to be fair to the KSU Extension group, it might have not made any difference if I had trimmed them and cleaned up the beds immediately. I just don't know. Over the summer, only two irises put up any blooms at all in my garden, and both were fall reblooming varieties. Lilac blooms just dried up and died, but the shrubs themselves survived. Strawberries, blackberries, apples, peaches bore not a single fruit that year (the freeze hit the strawberries as they were budding, and the peaches and apples were in full bloom). Viburnum 'Conoy' (*Viburnum burkwoodii* 'Conoy') was in a prominent spot at the end of the bed due to its evergreen nature, and it never leafed back out. A 'Henry's Garnet' sweetspire, and a 'Susan' magnolia also bit the dust. Variegated dogwoods and yellow-twig dogwood, all left the Earth behind. As I told my Dad, I had only planted peas and flowering sweet peas in the vegetable garden before The Freeze (Ide's of March and all that) and I'd never ever before seen a frost kill peas completely back to the ground, stems and all, but this year they did.

In all deference to Ms. Eddison, I became, after "The Freeze," what I now call a "Darwin Gardener." Like many of my fellow gardeners in this area last year, I had, by the end of May, 2007, given up on nursing lagging plants and coaxing stem health back with manure teas and incantations. I withdrew indoors from the summer heat and I cast my garden and its inhabitants upon the Fates to do with as they pleased. I was no longer a gardener of least resistance; I was a gardener of no resistance. Let natural selection take over, I reasoned, and I wouldn't face the pain again because the survivors in my garden would be those who could take any hit and keep on coming. It is a sure thing that I won't let a large part of my garden depend on irises for color again.

So, you ask, if I'm pledging my allegiance to Darwin, what plants did The Freeze help? There has to be a silver lining right? Well, those plants are few and far between. I must admit that the bee's balm (*Monarda didyma*) of which I have several cultivars including 'Prairie Night', 'Blue Stocking', 'Jacob Cline' and 'Gardenview Scarlet', all bloomed better than ever and spread in places I grow them, both later in 2007 and again this year in 2008. Note again that bee's balm is a native Kansas wildflower and probably very adapted to the vagarities of the prairie weather. The *Knautia macedonia* did and are doing well, and I must say that my worries about the Oakleaf Hydrangea (*Hydrangea quercifolia*) being winter hardy here were for naught as all three cultivars I grow have survived and thrived. Peonies, of course, did well as their iron-clad nature would suggest, even though they didn't bloom. All grasses and conifer evergreens survived as well (it's a prairie so, of course). To some extent and in some areas, my garden indeed went through a Darwinian process, with the feel and flavor of several beds being changed by plants which better survived The Freeze. If I only had confidence that the same plants will continue to thrive during the next ten year drought then I'd be a permanent convert to Darwinian conflict in the garden. But I'm afraid I'd be down to the one plant that does well in all Kansas weather: Wavy Leaf Thistle (*Cirsium undulatum*).

Extension Master Gardeners

Stemming from the Middle Ages, the term "Master" brings forth all kinds of respect, as it brings forth images of both a very skilled expert (as in a master craftsman) and also someone in authority (as in the Master of a ship). We all view a Chess Master (or Chess Grandmaster) as reaching the pinnacle of that sport. We refer to someone as Master if we follow their teachings or beliefs. To be labeled a "Master Gardener" sounds so very important, doesn't it? You've got a BS in horticulture or an MS in landscape design? Big deal, I'm an Extension Master Gardener. You're a Doctor (PhD) in plant pathology? Oh, you're not a real Doctor then. But, oh, to be a Master Gardener. Many horticultural authorities list that credential as their bona fides, including Paul James, HGTV's "The Gardener Guy." Just check the Internet for the many blogs who seem to feel that being a Master Gardener makes them a universal expert in all things green.

But, ask yourself, what does being an Extension Master Gardener really mean? Do you know? I, myself, lusted after the title for years. The local Extension Office held the training classes year after year on

Friday's in a given season, and due to work and the need to earn a living, I was unable to attend. Then finally, they announced a series of evening training sessions and I applied before the ink on the newspaper notice was dry. Finally I had my chance.

For the uninitiated, the Smith-Lever Act of 1914 created the Extension Service as part of the land grant colleges (themselves created by the Morrill Act in 1862) to serve as a means of disseminating the practical knowledge gained through agriculture research to the public. In 1972, a beleaguered Extension Service agent in the State of Washington reasoned that well-trained volunteers could respond to many of the everyday homeowner questions, freeing the Agent and his colleagues for more difficult problems, and he trained and certified the first Extension Master Gardeners. The Master Gardener Program has been a huge success and is now active in most states. Thus, the human drive to be held up and recognized for superior status was fiendishly harnessed to provide free help to county Extension Agents throughout America. And thousands of gardeners, myself included, have lined up and begged and worked for the, ahem, recognition.

Becoming an Extension Master Gardener (EMG) means that the individual has received some broad training (roughly forty to fifty class hours or the equivalent of about three hours of college credit) in the basics of soil structure, plant physiology, fertilization (relating both to propagation and nutrition of plants), pruning, pesticide application, lawn maintenance, landscape design, fruit production, and many other horticultural topics. In essence, EMG's gain just about enough knowledge to be dangerous, but luckily, many are already accomplished amateurs with some basic knowledge of the subjects. Classes are given by real local horticultural experts, often from an agricultural college or extension program. The night classes I took exemplified real effort on the part of these experts as it was also "after-hours" work for them and without extra pay to boot (and I have been told it won't be repeated again in the evenings for those reasons). In our classes, most of the instructors were excellent, entertaining, and obviously knowledgeable, including the handle-barred, dry-humored, gentleman who relished in talking about "floriferousness," the latter becoming a catch-phrase for my fellow EMG's. I, for one, was surprised and delighted by knowledge provided by the local city forester. A few seemed to have more specialized knowledge, able to identify a specific shrub in their slides, but not the flower pictured in front of it. To become an EMG also means that to be certified, you join a volunteer force with a significant initial time commitment to pay back the Extension Service for your classes (usually a matching number of hours as trained). It isn't the type of work you would expect. Very little of the work is performed, as I initially envisioned, in maintaining public gardens such as in centers of the traffic roundabouts which seem to be unfortunately proliferating throughout America (I would personally envision the best plantings in the roundabouts to be the bodies of the civil engineers who promote them). The county agents try to keep the volunteers focused on their educational purposes; teaching gardens at elementary schools, lawn-mower clinics, public demonstrations and 4-H judging. Once you're certified as a Master Gardener, you also have some annual minimal volunteer commitment and continuing education requirements or ethically you must stop using the title.

All actions have unforeseen consequences, and the astonishing consequence of taking the EMG course is not necessarily the training you receive, but the entrance into an entire different social network within the community. Quickly, I became acquainted with other gardeners from all walks and philosophies of life, from schoolteacher to tree-hugger, from businessperson to housewife. All are passionate volunteers, and all of them become as close as parishioners in doing work all over the community. Like all new acquaintances, some fellow EMG's are maddening and some become your best friends. I've seen EMG committee members work together for results far beyond expectations, and I've seen EMG committees where everyone seems to have a different idea about what should be done. In my own garden, I've had fellow Master Gardeners who come to see the roses and others who believe the buffalo grass is the most important feature of the garden. But as Master Gardener's, we're all experts and therefore all correct, aren't we?

In fact, that brings up another "benefit" of being a Master Gardener; sooner or later your personal garden is sure to be on the list for the annual Garden Tour. My garden, as a matter of fact, is on the tour this very year as I write this.

Soil Sorrow

Any group of essays about gardening in the Flint Hills would be amiss if it didn't also address the soil that we garden on. After purchasing land, I visited the local county office in search of soil maps to determine what types of soil I could expect on the property. The soil on these hills is usually a combination of "Benfield-Florence" soil and in the lower regions "Breaks-Alluvial." Benfield-Florence soil is described as having a clay-loam top of six to ten inches thick and then a roughly two foot layer of mixed clay loam and chert. What that means is that in real life, the ridge tops are composed of about six to twelve inches of good brown topsoil. That top layer has lots of really nice organic matter mixed in. Beneath that is a foot-thick layer of mixed flint and limestone known as chert, packed together with brown sticky clay as a barrier to anything, including roots and fence posts that tries to penetrate it. Below that is alkaline orange clay ranging between one and three feet thick to limestone bedrock. Nothing grows in the orange clay but geodes.

According to the soil catalogue, this soil has moderate to slow moisture permeability (meaning I can expect a lot of rain runoff on the slopes and little soaking in). Alas, the worst news is that I was going to try to garden on soil that the soil experts informed me was "not suited to cultivated crops," but was "excellent for openland wildlife." In other words, it probably couldn't be farmed for sustenance (as the westward settlers of the last century discovered), but I could count on lots of deer and rabbits to invade my garden. Has a clearer message questioning one's gardening sanity ever been sent? But, as a new landowner, I was in my see-no-evil, hear-no-evil mode. In my exuberant blindness, I only wondered whether cultivated crops included roses and garden perennials. I should have taken a hint from the list of the trees and bushes that were expected to grow well in the area. The trees listed included Cottonwood, Silver maple, Sycamore, Burr Oak, Honeylocust, Osage orange, Russian Mulberry, and Russian Olive. In most gardening guides, these would be listed as scrub and undesirable trees; in fact, although I haven't listened, local nursery workers have tried to dissuade me from buying both Sycamore and Cottonwood because of their general "messiness". Most of these trees, particularly the Honeylocust and Osage orange, would grow on solid rock if need be and that's actually a benefit in my soil. The bushes recommended in the soil treatise included fragrant sumac, gray dogwood, bush honeysuckle and lilac. Well, at least I knew the last was a desirable garden plant.

In moving here and purchasing land, I immediately set out to fence in my newly purchased property. Fencing for my planned cattle baron phase necessitated barb wire, steel T-posts, and good solid end posts. I hired two young workers to help me set the end posts and rented a BobCat with a post-hole digger attached. On the first day we set up to dig all the corner posts and started with a corner at the north ridgeline. It ultimately took the three of us all day to dig three postholes even with the mechanized equipment because on the north ridge near my house, you have six inches of topsoil and two feet of chert mixed with clay (as expected with Benfield-Florence soil). The rest of the fence luckily went a little easier and we were able to dig the corner holes in the lower valley and up on the other ridge in another couple of days, and in a few weeks of work alone I was able to drive the T-posts by hand and string the wire. I did find it disconcerting however to occasionally drive a steel T-post and have it bend on a rock and end up coming back up out of the ground.

If you're planning to plant trees or shrubs in the Flint Hills, you essentially have several choices. The first choice is to use both a spade and a pickaxe or a maul. The spade, if sharp, will cut down the first foot or so. Particularly if you jump on it repeatedly with both feet. I've had planting sessions where I've ended up with the arches of both feet bruised and sore for several days. It's not the soil that's hard (unless it's a drought period); it's the grass roots that have to be cut. After that first foot it's best to use the pickaxe to loosen up the chert and clay and then remove it by hand. Softening the soil with water makes it worse; the clay just compacts, cements the chert together, and gets slimy to boot. The second choice to make a planting hole is to haul in good topsoil, make a raised berm, and then plant in the berm. That one works pretty well if you have money, but it'd be about as effective to just pile the dollar bills down and plant in them. The third choice is to use dynamite to make the holes, but that isn't the best choice because you have a tendency to compact soil at the sides of the hole too much and the Federal Bureau of Alcohol, Tobacco, and Firearms may want pay you a visit (which didn't work out well at Ruby Ridge so I'd like to avoid it).

Flint Hills gardeners are therefore not keen on the usual recommendation to make the hole for a tree or shrub the depth of the root ball and twice the diameter. We tend to be of the hard love school of gardening; squeezing each plant into a hole marginally big enough for the root ball and then the plant is on its own. That philosophy has arisen because any excess digging in this soil sends a Kansas gardener from merely being tired to being exhausted and dehydrated. It's hard enough to make diameter of the hole big enough for a one gallon potted plant in my soil. I've planted trees where the pile of rocks removed from the hole equals the size of the root ball. In fact, I planted an 'October Glory' maple (*Acer rubrum* 'October Glory) in exactly that situation last year between the road and the house. The county Extension Agent and I have a bet going as to whether it will stunt the tree or not. Directly opposite it I have planted a Paperbark Maple (*Acer griseum*) that I have more hope for because it had a whole eighteen inches of topsoil before I hit the chert. Of course, the hole for the maple was essentially a dry clay pot the diameter of the root ball when I planted it, but I trust in the gardening deities that the roots will penetrate the sides and grow into the surrounding topsoil, if not into the chert.

We justify our small holes by convincing ourselves that the roots will grow better if they meet the real soil right away instead of becoming soft and lax in fake soft well-draining filler topsoil. I try to tell myself that I buy the smallest plants I can find because I'm cheap and that they'll grow to make up the size differential anyway within a few years. In reality, I buy the smallest plants I can find because I can dig a smaller hole and I'm cheap and by the time I exhaust myself digging the hole, I usually don't care if they grow. There are several nurseries in the area that don't get my business because they sell more expensive plants in three gallon containers. A three gallon container hole takes me a spade, a pry bar and upwards of an hour to dig on the upper levels of my land. If that's all they have, I look elsewhere for the smaller pot.

I also have a tendency to reuse holes because of the difficulty of starting new ones. If I plant something and it dies, I don't consider altering the landscape design or worrying about any disease or imbalance of the soil. The next plant is going right back in the same hole because I know there won't be any rock to go through when planting. I do try to learn why the first plant died before placing the second, though, and it's always useful information to dig up a plant that should have been placed in arid soil and find that it's sitting in a swimming pool of water trapped by the clay. Or to pull up a root ball and find out I didn't spread the roots out enough when planted and the roots have become "pot-bound" in my clay soil, trapped within the original soil because they couldn't penetrate the clay to the sides.

In total, I've probably made a few thousand holes in my landscape and garden and I've become accustomed to the difficulty and usually only procrastinate a week until I get out the spade for a new hole. I find that the time period between when a plant stored in the garage starts to yellow and before it actually loses its leaves is the best time to balance the plant's needs with my own reluctance to tackle digging.

If I've got one thing to be proud of in my own garden, it's that my soil does seem to be hospitable to earthworms, at least in the garden beds. I can't sink a spade anymore anywhere in the vegetable garden or the perennial beds without hitting a nice *Lumbricus terrestris* or dumping it out into the open. I'm always careful with these worms, placing them gently back into my plantings and make sure there's enough room between the flint pieces for them to move around in the planting hole. Digging enough worms for a fishing trip is the matter of minutes as long as one doesn't go into the chert layer beneath all my beds. Because of either the thick hay mulch or the earthworms or both, I notice that my bed soils drain really well after a couple of years of cultivation, unlike the primary clay with which I began.

I've become so accustomed to the Kansas soil, I've forgotten that there are actually areas of good native soil on the planet. A year or so back I purchased a 'Josee' repeat-blooming Lilac (*Syringa pubescens spp. microphylla* 'Josee') to give to my father for his birthday. On a trip home to Indiana I grabbed a spade and went to plant it for him. Following my usual pattern, I jumped on the spade hard with both feet. The spade sunk into the ground up to the handle and I felt like my head was going to slam into my boots. I had entirely forgotten that Indiana soil is real honest-to-god sandy loam down as far as I've ever dug and that the hand-pumped well in my father's vegetable garden was hand-driven down to water level. For the lilac, I dug a nice five gallon hole into soft sandy moist soil in about twenty seconds, planted the lilac, and walked away. Today, it's about twice the size of either of the Josee's I grow here. Life is hard in Kansas.

Fragrance in the Garden

The longer I garden, the more I appreciate fragrances of all types in the garden. I believed for ages that I had to search out different plants primarily for their unique attractive qualities and the beauty added to the garden by their presence, whether by color or form or flower. I was selecting plants to provide what I term as the symphony of the garden; not flowering in an overwhelming crescendo, but with refrains and echoes here and there throughout the garden and the seasons. But lately, I have realized that while I'm sometimes consciously neglecting the other four God-given senses of sound, smell, touch and taste, my subconscious has not been nearly so negligent. In fact, beneath the concerto of bloom in my garden is a second quieter symphony of scent that plays in accent to the sense of sight. This season it's the honeysuckle that weaves its quiet harmony, the next it's the rose. Many of my early aromatic garden discoveries were happy accidents, but I now have learned to seek out plants that will add their special scents to the garden as well as their beauty, and within a species, those individual cultivars that will best perfume the air around them. Fragrance and beauty are not mutually exclusive, and the attentive gardener can pay tribute and cultivate both within the garden.

There are entire books written on fragrant plants and dealing with scent within the garden, but I shall not even attempt to be all inclusive here. Rather, I intend to list those few species that I can no longer garden without because of the joy they bring. Each of the plants discussed hither sound a clear note at a different time and place in my garden, but together they create a bouquet that lasts through the season.

In point of fact, the entire idea for this essay arose because of a single plant blooming now, at the start of fall, in my garden. I was outside working this week and noticed I was smelling candy on the air and relishing in it. My senses alerted, and my pleasure center engaged, I began to hunt for the source. Nose in the air, I moved this way and that, discerning where the wind was coming from and probably appearing to the outside observer to act just as a Brittany Spaniel during a hunt. And in a short time, hundreds of feet away, I knew for certain the source; the Sweet Autumn Clematis (*Clematis paniculata*) growing in the center of my hydrangea bed was blooming and was perfuming my entire yard. There are some sweet odors I think are overbearing. Oriental lilies come to mind as one that a single flower in a closed room is too strong an odor for me. I can't, for instance, eat if there is an Oriental lily blossom in a kitchen arrangement, but *Clematis paniculata* is one aroma that I can't get enough of and could overdose on if possible. I'm not a scent scientist and don't even pretend to know the language of fragrance, but I'd describe the perfume as a mixture of sugar, honey, and vanilla tones, with just a bit of a muskier underbelly.

The Sweet Autumn Clematis is in many other respects a perfect plant as well. Mine sits in the middle of my garden, growing at will on a tall (10 foot high) cylinder of woven wire. Two years old, this vine has made it to the seven foot level, completely filling the cylinder and now completely covering it with the small white star-shaped blossoms that carry the real treasure. It is a white tower in the center of the bed. It grows here in my Zone 5B garden completely without care, receiving no extra water throughout the summer. It has no insect pests of fungal diseases that I have found, although earlier today I noticed a June Bug (ggrrrrhhh) had been attracted to its aroma, and the foliage remains perfect from spring through fall. In my humble opinion (IMHO for those of the internet age) God rested on the seventh day and on the eighth day, refreshed, he gave us the Sweet Autumn Clematis.

My scented year currently begins in the spring with an accidental scent discovery, the purple-leaf honeysuckle (*Lonicera japonica* 'Purpurea'). I had planted a number of this particular honeysuckle as a groundcover for an exposed bank of soil on the west side of my yard at the beginning of our time here. Since the steep bank was composed primarily of flint rock and anaerobic clay, I was searching for something that could survive the conditions and prevent me from having to mow it, and I settled on the purple-leaf form because of its low-growing nature and because I was in my purple-foliage phase of garden growth (you know, the one where you can't resist any purple-foliaged plant cultivar, no matter how hideous it is or poorly it grows?). I hadn't thought of the scent being an advantage because frankly, honeysuckle is one of those plants that others may be better able to appreciate than me. I've had access to a number of other *Lonicera* species and for most of them, I have to be nose-in-blossom to really appreciate the fragrance. But with 'Purpurea', my spring is welcomed with a light sweet fragrance that the west wind spreads throughout the yard at will. Currently, the honeysuckle completely clothes a piece of hillside approximately 80X25 feet with a purple-green mass most of the year, and for several weeks provides me with a slice of heaven. Despite my leaving behind my "purple period", and despite the fact that I hope the award for first spring fragrance is soon taken instead by a witch hazel (*Hamamelis intermedia* 'Jelena') I planted earlier this year, this honeysuckle has earned a permanent place in my landscape for combining both utility and pleasure.

Shortly after the honeysuckle blooms for me, another delicate scent permeates the air in the vicinity of my home, the scent of fragrant viburnums. This one is due to several fragrant viburnum species and cultivars I grow, chief among which are *Viburnum burkwoodii*, *Viburnum fragrans* 'Mohawk and *Viburnum juddii*. These all carry the most fragrant, delicate white-shaded-to-pink blooms in spring, and again, it's the sweet scent of these flowers that keep me holding on to these gangly bushes. It's hard to reconcile the massive nature of these bushes with the tantalizing delicate scent, but these plants match the picture of a gentle giant for the garden. I have one 'Mohawk' near the front walk of the house, greeting visitors as they arrive and available to freshen the dining room if the windows are open, and I have another in the back of the garden to bring in the aroma from another direction. In fact, as I think about it, no matter which direction the wind blows here, between the 'Mohawk's' and the *V. juddii*, the scent from one or the other is always directed across the center of the garden. Now that's accidental plant placement at its best!

One plant that most gardeners seeking fragrance often neglect is the Sweetbriar rose of Shakespearean times, *Rosa eglanteria*, also labeled by the plant name relabelers in some texts as *Rosa rubiginosa*. By either name, this is a six to nine foot towering and intensely thorny shrub which bears insignificant pale pink five-petaled blossoms in the spring. The blossoms themselves are not particularly fragrant, but the surprise of this plant is that the foliage itself bears the most delicious green apple scent when crushed or when wet by dew or rain. God forbid that most of us should court lightning by gardening during thunderstorms, but throughout the spring, summer and fall, anytime there's high humidity in Kansas (which is always) or a light drizzle is falling, this shrub perfumes an entire corner of my yard. As an added bonus, this rose does double duty and bears a plethora of spiny orange rose hips throughout the winter, or at least till the birds remove them all. And there's always the possibility of a third landscape function for this thorny citadel. My prickly specimen is placed out of the way in a bed dedicated to shrub roses, but this is one rose that if planted beneath a window near the house will live up to its brier name and could serve three functions; perfume, winter beauty, and protection from prowlers. More than once, when removing leaves to crush and accent the fragrance for visitors, I've been bitten merely brushing this plant. I'd hate to be the burglar or teenage suitor to try to make it past the sweet smell of the foliage. Excuse me, that reminds me that I need to plant one beneath my daughter's window soon.

There are of course, other plants which bloom over the seasons and entertain my olfactory senses. I could wax melodious on the qualities of the various mockoranges, of which I grow two that bloom at different times, *Philadelphus x virginalis* 'Virginal' in May and *Philadelphus lewisii* 'Blizzard' in June. I could discuss at length the delicate scent of the flowering almond *Prunus glandulosa* 'Rosea' that borders my front walkway. And there are, of course, the many and varied cultivars of lilac that dot my landscape, from the *Syringa vulgaris* cultivars such as 'Sensation', 'Wonderblue.' 'Edith Cavell' and 'Yankee Doodle' to the dwarf Korean lilac *Syringa meyer,* cutleaf lilac *Syringa lacinata* and on to the reblooming modern hybrids such as 'Josee'. All in all, I grow about twelve different varieties that provide a month's worth of lilac bloom for my pleasure.

Not Enough Grasses

I have decided that I need more ornamental grasses in my garden. In fact, I think ornamental grasses are the most underutilized landscape and garden plants in the Great Plains area. Further, ornamental grasses are probably underrepresented in gardens across the United States. Need I go on?

There is certainly a national movement towards incorporating ornamental grass species in our perennial beds, whether in large groups or mixed beds. Most enlightened gardeners have probably already heeded the words of the "experts" and added a grass clump or two in their gardens so that they may be seen by others as standing clearly in the forefront of garden thought and design. Well, hogwash. A clump here or a clump there is not a garden revolution and it is not the best use of these plants in our gardens. We must confront our mistakes and forge onward to plant these pinnacles of Pleistocene evolution.

Speaking for myself, I can provide a number of reasons why I haven't used more grasses, but I think my main lack of motivation is three-fold, and all three are wrong. First, I have in the past bemoaned the lack of flowers on the grasses and their green blob-like presence in the garden, which slowly grows taller and wider as the summer goes on. Second, they really don't look like much after you put them into the garden. Third and finally, *Calamagrostis acutiflora* 'Karl Foerster' is one of the most touted landscape grasses with widespread availability.

My awakening to grasses came today as a result of the realization that in fact, grasses are a flowering plant, but they're a fall flowering plant. They dependably provide colorful flowers, albeit usually white flowers, just as the sedums, asters, and other previous fall mainstays do. Face it, neither phlox nor hydrangea is any more showy in the garden than a solid mature clump of *Miscanthus sinensis* 'Gracillimus' in full bloom. And what provides better autumn color than the red leaves and white flowers of M. *sinensis* 'purpurascens' in the garden? Answer; nothing, particularly as I've got it placed in prominence next to 'Tiger Eyes' sumac (*Rhus typhine* 'Tiger Eyes') and it makes a spectacular focal point in the fall.

Even better, set the flowers aside and let's consider the foliage. Yes, I've got to agree that the descriptions of the bluer grasses and some of the variegated grasses is a little exaggerated in terms of their actual impact on the garden. Most grasses, no matter how much we wish to call them blue, never really reach much past faintly blue-green. It's sort of a daylily-like interpretation of grass colors. Just like all apricot, peach, and melon daylilies look orange from a distance, most grasses, whether blue, green, or in between, all look blue-green at a distance. But blue-green is not the end of the grass foliage. There are variegated forms such as M. *sinensis* 'Rigoletto', M. *sinensis* 'variegatis', or *Phalaris arundinacea* 'Strawberries and Cream' that are plenty light enough to provide silver-white focal points in my garden. And even among the silvers, the forms are different as the 'Strawberries and Cream' is short (about two foot tall in my garden) and sprawling while the 'Rigoletto' is upright and taller (about five foot). And other new forms of Maiden Grass such as 'Gold Bar' (M. sinensis 'Gold Bar') don't need to be looked at closely to see the bands on the leaves. 'Gold Bar' is like looking at a tiger in the garden. And despite my complaints about color nomenclature, my Blue Lyme grass (*Elymus glaucus*) really is blue to my eyes. As proof of the color, when this invasive grass escapes the double plastic pots I've got it planted in within the ground, it's very easy to spot in the garden as it attempts to spread to the horizon. It's just that it spreads faster than the gardener can run to pull it up.

And of course, grasses, no matter the variety, give us one aspect to our gardens without fail; movement. Landscape designers and plants-people of all stripes wax philosophical about the addition of movement to the garden provided by grasses in the wind. And if you think that sounds good for a California garden, just try it in Kansas. Grasses are the cat's meow for a Kansas Garden. We don't have water features, unless they're plopped on the landscape like an artificial puddle of urine, but we do have plenty of wind to motor the grasses. We just have to hope our grasses don't whip themselves to death before they can grow. In fact, during a seminar recently where an ornamental grass expert from southern Kansas was proclaiming the delights of the 'Prince' and 'Princess' Napiergrass (*Pennisetum purpureum)*, one of the participants spoke up to point out that her specimens were less than perfect as they were broken and split by the wind. As both these varieties are hardy only to Zone 8 and annuals here, I've got two reasons to stay away from those varieties.

My grass-deficient justification that grasses don't provide much for looks after they're in the garden is simply a matter of inexperience and lack of faith in catalogue descriptions. It is true that most grasses won't look like much in the first, or second or sometimes even third year after you plant them. Then, at some point around that third year after planting, they bloom in September when the roses are bare from blackspot and you find your eye drawn to them time and time again across the garden. Suddenly, those stringy skinny ugly ducklings fill out like a young girl during puberty and you come back to school in the fall to find them suddenly irresistible, even captivating, where before they were merely a dull part of the scenery. The ones with good bloom, like many of the *Miscanthus,* are downright voluptuous now with their newfound display. And some of the ones without good bloom glow red in the fall as if wearing makeup for the first time and they make up for their lack of bloom and you forgive them for their classic beauty. And the grasses that sprawl loosely around the garden, draping themselves over everything else, well, those are like the girls you don't bring home to mother and although they may have their uses, we don't choose to help them multiply across the garden.

I'm right, though, about the 'Karl Foerster'. The popularity of Karl among landscape designers is as incomprehensible to me as the popularity of purple barberry and lime-green spirea among those same wretched creatures. I view its only real saving grace as the fact that it is used often enough to break up the barberry-spirea monotony. This Feather Reed grass (*Calamagrostis acutiflora* 'Karl Foerster') was the labeled the 2001 Perennial Plant of the Year by the Perennial Plant Association (whatever that is) and is variously described as being a "vertical masterpiece," providing "wonderful contrast amongst low shrubs and perennials'" and "one of the most versatile, attractive, and low maintenance ornamental grasses." All this populous breath is wasted, in my mind, on a plant that is dull green, stiff as a board, and which has small straight sticklike blooms that turn brown before I can see the slightest pink tinge that is described by others. The foliage develops no fall color other than tan and although it's true that, as in the words of one writer, "the flowers often remain erect despite heavy snowfall," I find myself wishing that the flowers would do something, anything, to break their stiff monotony. It's also described as the "metamorphic" or "perpetual motion" grass, as if the fact that it sways in the wind was unique among grasses. Maybe this drought-tolerant and clay-soil-tolerant plant just doesn't do well in the Kansas climate. It certainly doesn't do anything in my garden. But if so, why do local designers plant it everywhere, traffic roundabouts, focal specimens, and house foundations? I pointed it out to my wife just this morning, where it was part of the landscaping at IHOP. Green, stiff, and boring.

For God's sake, let's pick a grass to promote that will really excite the public, maybe *M. sinensis* 'Gracillimus' with its bountiful bloom, or even *M. sinensis* 'Graziella', which perhaps doesn't have quite as outstanding a bloom as 'Gracillimus', but makes up for it with a translucent red/gold fall foliage color that glows in the setting sunlight. Or even *M. sinensis* 'Morning Light' with its thin silvery foliage. Or *Panicum virgatum* 'Northwind' if we want a tall upright grass. Or, if we must have a Calamagrostis, then choose *C. acutiflora* 'Eldorado' which has much nicer gold-striped foliage, or C. *acutiflora* 'Overdam' , a variety that has better flowers than 'Foerster'. Is it really too much to ask if we dismiss the popular for the actually beautiful?

The Home and Garden Television Network

One would think that a television network entitled Home and Garden Television or HGTV, would be about 50% split between home maintenance and decoration or between garden shows. Well, one would primarily be wrong. One of my current beefs with life in general and television in particular is that there is precious little real gardening on the HGTV channel. In fact, only two shows occur regularly; *Gardening by the Yard* with Paul James "The Gardener Guy" twice a week or so (and many of those are reruns) and once a week, *The Gardener's Diary* with Erica Glasener (which currently seem to be new episodes, or at least they're new to me). And both are on in the very early morning here in the central time zone (6:30 a.m. on Sunday and 6:00 a.m. on Thursday). Somehow national networks have gotten the idea that all gardeners get up with the sun and only watch TV while the dew is on the grass (and I'd point out that if I lived on the Pacific Coast, my only chance to see these shows would be around 4:00 a.m.). For God's sake, doesn't anyone think a gardener might like to sleep in on Sunday? Both are great shows, but please, get real.

Oh, I know, the programmers and broadcasters would claim there are a number of other gardening shows available on the channel. I don't count landscaping shows that primarily transform someone's suburban back yard into a gravel, barberry, and spirea paradise as a gardening show. And there are about six or seven of those landscaping shows on, and all of them are at a more civil time period than the real gardening shows. Don't try to fool me either; the show entitled *The City Gardener* is really just a show about someone who landscapes small city backyards. *Rebecca's Garden* doesn't count either; most of its episodes are about decorating or landscaping, not planting or plants. In fact, I see more episodes about gardening on the local PBS channel than I see on HGTV.

Please, God, or whoever controls HGTV, give us gardeners a break. Show us plant collectors in the Himalayas, botanical gardens of the world, even (Lord Help Us) Roger Swain in his vegetable garden. Show them at a decent hour so we have a real excuse to skip church on Sunday morning or to come home early on Saturday evenings. How about a show series featuring biographies of famous past gardeners (you could get double mileage by rerunning episodes on The Biography Channel)? How about a show touring famous large private or public gardens, such as Winterthur or Longwood Gardens hosted by Erica Glasener or some other equally luscious persona? How about a series of episodes about gardening obsessions; giant pumpkin growers, rose show fanatics, or orchid breeders (which could likely also do double duty on America's Funniest Home Videos)? Or, if these shows already exist, give us reruns or the opportunity to purchase copies of reruns at least? Gardening hasn't changed that much over the years. Even a show hosted by Gertrude Jekyll in silent movie form might be worthwhile and preferable to yet another show that makes a candlestick holder out of old bottles decorated with sugar and pencil erasers. There used to be a series on HGTV called "*The Winter Gardener*", that I only caught a few of before it was discontinued, but it had some great episodes, among which was one featuring one of Lauren Springer Ogden's early gardens in the foothills of Colorado. Sadly, these are unavailable, either as reruns or as taped shows. Anybody out there want to digitize the videos to these shows and make a fortune?

Of the two existing <u>real</u> gardening shows available on HGTV, I watch both, dragging myself up from sound slumber to make sure I don't miss an important episode of either. The zany Paul James is very entertaining in *Gardening by the Yard* and this show has the added benefit of being taped in Oklahoma, near enough to my Kansas garden to provide for similar plants and climates to compare. Many of the more mundane segments are basic gardening technique oriented and are placed in his own yard, but those are still interesting and helpful. In the case of my "Easter Island" statue, a cement head casted in the visage of one of the Easter Island originals, the show was very helpful because my wife had made fun of the statue in my yard right up until we saw one on the show in Paul's yard. I have discounted her current hypothesis that Paul and I both chose the statue only because we're red state rednecks. Paul James also has interesting guests, some of them repeat guests such as the wacky Ciscoe Morris, and he creates unusual segments of the show on occasion that highlight techniques for other areas of the country, exotic or new garden species or methods, and notable gardens far and wide. Of course, gardeners who have no real interest in Paul's Zone 6 Oklahoma garden can simply watch the show to see what off-the-wall thing Paul does next. Besides, how could I not like the show? Paul, like myself, has obtained his Master Gardener Certification, albeit twenty-five years prior to me.

Of much higher standards is Erica Glasener's *The Gardener's Diary.* Each episode highlights a different garden and in a different area of the country as Erica takes us on a tour through these amateur's gardens along with their creators. Gardens featured in the show have all different styles and emphasis on different plants and the overall tone of the show is one of good taste and refinement. As much as by the gardens, however, most of the good taste and refinement of the show is manifested by Erica, herself. Seemingly, by her accent, which was stronger on the earlier shows, Erica is a former (or present since I know her only through her show and writings) Southern Belle and she looks and acts the part to perfection. And I am a born sucker for southern accents, weakened genetically by my Y-chromosome to pay complete attention and deference to any female voice dripping with honey. In older episodes, from the previous season or two, she played the part even better as she almost always appeared in a sun dress and nice large straw sun bonnet, blond manes aflow beneath the brim of the hat and accent flowing. It was Rebecca of Sunnybrook Farm meets haite couture high society. In the most recent episodes she seems to have lost the sun bonnet, acquired emancipation in the form of trading the sun dress for blue jeans, and trimmed the blond locks, but if the overall effect is of more maturity, it is no less stunning. My wife seems vaguely threatened that I would wake up specifically to catch the weekly episode, a feeling that was not diminished recently when after watching one episode my main recollection was of Erica reclining for a moment in a shaded hammock as featured on that particular show. I would have been able to defend myself better if I could have recalled under interrogation a single plant placed around the hammock, but of course they were all mundane things and beneath recollection. I should admit that I watch the show partially to see the gardens and partially to spend at least one morning a week waking up with Erica on the screen. But I won't, because it's just possible my wife may stick it out and read this far into the book. She'll probably understand, though. Gardening, at the core, is about beauty and life, is it not? And just because a middle-aged man admires a fellow gardener's style, that's not any reason to not speak to him for upwards of two weeks. Don't you agree Honey? Honey? Sweetie?

The World's Ten Best Roses

Having portrayed myself as a rose snob and connoisseur, I felt it was my duty to lay out for you, the reader, what I would choose, in a completely impartial way, as the ten best roses of the world. Alas, having undertaken it, I now find this self-challenge to be of a very difficult nature due to the added imposition that I must remain impartial in my choices. To rectify this predicament, in the true manner of Western politicians regardless of political bent, I'm instead going to just run with it and let my personal biases have a heyday. And in all deference to David Letterman, I'm giving the list from one to ten, rather than as a suspenseful countdown.

Before I attempt the list, however, I will disclose some of those aforementioned biases in the interests of convincing the reader that my tastes are supreme and should be unquestioned hither forward. I have previously alluded (see the chapter titled "Rose Snob") to the cold hard fact that Hybrid Tea, Floribunda, and Grandiflora roses are completely inferior in all respects to their ancestors and that all the eugenics of rose breeding after 1867 have served only to weaken the Genus. Although there are exceptions, where the aim of breeders has been to return hardiness and grace to the rose such as in those magnificent hybrids by the late Dr. Griffith Buck of Iowa State University, most of the modern breeders have sold their souls to the commercial taskmaster, introducing roses like this year's new car models and, in fact, often naming them in the same bourgeois fashion. I'm not a fan in general of many modern hybrids, and I count among those...gasp...the David Austin English rose hybrids. While David's motives to return to the older form and delicious fragrances of the roses while keeping modern color advancements intact are admirable, the end result in my Zone 5 sun-stricken world is often a rose that struggles or has only fleeting beauty. I grow several of the Austin introductions, my favorite among them being 'Heritage', but I can include none of them in my ten best list. In fact, my preference for the Buck roses in contrast to the English roses may simply be the result of the fact that Griffith Buck's selection process occurred nearby in Iowa, while the English roses are selected for performance in a cooler, wetter, more stable climate than my own. In that vein, I disdain having to protect roses for the harsh Zone 5 winters of northeastern Kansas, and thus I am biased towards hardier cultivars and species of roses such as the Rugosa crosses, the Ag Canada introductions, and the Old Garden Roses. All the roses which follow are hardy with no or minimal winter protection in my garden.

The World's Numero Uno best rose, without doubt, is the white damask 'Madame Hardy'. I have spoken elsewhere (again see the section titled "Rose Snob") of her immeasurable qualities, the perfect flower form, delicious fragrance, vase-like garden silhouette and the hint of warmer color in new blossoms, so I won't repeat it here. If she was a woman, I'd marry her. If she was a dog, I'd feed her only the best gravy. If she was a plant...well, she is and so I will worship her and nourish her and fertilize her (so to speak). I grow three of Madame Hardy, spacing them throughout the garden so as to both increase my enjoyment of her and lessen the chances that all three are wiped out in the same calamity, but I will admit that her placement straight in front of the first window I look out of every morning is no accident. During her three-week bloom period, I linger by that window every morning, timing the peak of her floriferousness so that I can overindulge in the luxury of perfection at its peak.

My second rose choice might be an unusual one on the surface, for I would choose a species rose of dubious single flower as my second best. That rose is *Rosa eglanteria*, also known as *R. rubiginosa*, the Sweet Briar rose of Shakespearian fame. Native to Europe, this rose carries foliage perfumed with none other than the scent of apples, a fragrance elicited either by crushing the leaves or by merely being in the vicinity of the bush during a rain. I almost never pass the bush with grabbing a few leaves and inhaling them into my olfactory passages. I've also been known to exit the house during a light rain, leading my sweet wife and family to call into question my sanity at times, but it's merely a compulsion to sample the delicious air I know I will find in the back corner of my garden. Pneumonia be damned, there is heaven in the vicinity of my back rose bed. *R. eglanteria* is in form a rather large (eight to twelve foot) coarse bush with undistinguished single light pink flowers. It does form a good number of orange hips to provide some fall and winter interest, but it's the foliage glands that make this rose one to have and keep. There are a few hybrids of *R. eglanteria* described that might have been better in flower form, but most or all have evidently been lost to history.

The third rose that I would place for judgment by my peers would be the little-known Rugosa rose 'Marie Bugnet'. Bred by Frenchman turned Canadian George Bugnet (pronounced boo-nay) in 1973, Marie Bugnet is a hardy cross of the roses Therese Bugnet and F. J. Grootendorst. The result is a lovely, continuous flowering, white, double, very fragrant rose of compact (about four foot around), and bushy, completely disease-free growth. She is self-cleaning (always a good characteristic in a beautiful female) and will retain a number of fat orange hips for winter interest. I grow approximately thirty of the *R. rugosa* hybrids and Marie Bugnet is the best of the bunch. All of those great characteristics put her at least in the honorable mention category for rosarians, but it is one distinguishing quality that places her as my number three. She is the earliest rose to bloom in my garden every year, and thus she welcomes the rose season for me and I love her and hold her up for that simple act. I've read in other texts that she's the first to bloom in other areas of the country as well, so I can recommend her without reservation to help my fellow rose-lovers leave their winters behind. How do you get one? Search, my friend, search.

Number four on my list of best roses would have to be the Bourbon 'Zephirine Drouhin'. I'm not alone in this choice, as she is one of the highest rated roses in commerce, and I know that our local county extension agent believes her to be the perfect rose. Introduced in France in 1868, Zephirine stands tall in the rose garden, a climber reaching to about eight feet in my garden, but said to go over ten feet elsewhere. She is a pink rose of semi-double form, and she has all the delicious fragrance of her Bourbon ancestry in spades. She's vigorous and hardy, needing no protection in my Zone 5 climate and she has good disease resistance as well, needing little spraying for blackspot. She repeat blooms with confidence over the summer, doling out her blossoms in careful numbers so as not to overwhelm the admirer. As added enticement for some gardeners she likes to be tied up a bit before she'll perform best. She'll also perform better than most other roses in partial shade, where she can be appreciated at the cool leisure of the gardener without fear of sunburn on a hot summer day. Topping this collage of perfection though, she is thornless, giving form to the ancient question of "what would a rose be without its thorns?" The answer is that it would be Zephirine Drouhin, a true fragrant beauty anywhere that the sun strikes a few hours a day.

My fifth rose is a shakeup of the gardening establishment, the shrub rose 'Carefree Beauty'. Carefree Beauty is a pink, semi-double, continuous blooming shrub rose that was bred by the late Dr. Griffith Buck, professor of horticulture at Iowa State University. Dr. Buck began a rose breeding program in 1949 aimed at creating a line of roses which were cane hardy in the Iowa Zone 4 climate. Using crosses from *R. laxa* and a sweetbrier cultivar named 'Josef Rothmund', Dr. Buck inadvertently also bred tremendous disease resistance into his crosses by growing them after the first year in the open garden without aid of disease prevention sprays. The results were over ninety roses eventually introduced to commerce, with some of them introduced after his death by his widow and daughter. I grow a number of great Buck cultivars, including yellow 'Prairie Harvest', white 'Prairie Star', amber 'Winter Sunset', pink 'Quietness', and fuchsia-pink 'Earth Song', but if pressed, I believe the best Buck cultivar for any garden would be 'Carefree Beauty'. This rose was one of the first chosen by the Texas A&M Department of Horticulture as an Earth Kind® rose, designated for its trouble-free, disease free nature and one of only fifteen roses currently selected. It also gained fame as one of the most disease-free roses collected by the Texas Rose Rustlers, who gave it the study name 'Katy Road Pink' before determining its ultimate identity. Carefree Beauty is one rose that I never spray for blackspot and it retains its perfect leaves all through summer, as well as blooming continuously in a clear pink and then leaving behind plenty of bright orange hips to last through the winter. If 'Madame Hardy' is the gorgeous royal princess of the garden, 'Carefree Beauty' is the rosy-cheeked peasant handmaiden who does the work.

With my sixth choice, I must promote another climber, but yet one with a twist. A miniature climber, 'Jeanne Lajoie' is quite deserving of this list and of placement into your garden. Jeanne Lajoie is a climbing miniature rose growing to about six to eight feet in stature in my garden. I have her placed against a rock wall on the east side of the house where she keeps her legs and feet hidden behind a Mugo pine (*Pinus mugo*), and raises her head covered with pink blossoms for all passersby. She is a clear cool pink with perfect, if tiny, hybrid-tea form and she never is without a few blooms to greet admirers. Bred in only 1975 and thus scarcely thirty-eight years old as this is written, Jeanne Lajoie has achieved worldwide fame and was designated with the American Rose Society Award of Excellence as a toddler in 1977 and added to the Miniature Rose Hall of Fame in 2001. At one time, she was the highest rated rose by the American Rose Society, and she seems perfectly at home across the United States as well as hardy in many of the northern climes.

At number seven, we return to our roots as snobbish rosarians and we must add the prima sexpot of the Albas, the ancient 'Great Maiden's Blush' to our list. Maiden's Blush is a blush-pink alba of large stature, once-blooming each summer, but in great numbers and with such a voluptuous presence in the June garden that she draws all eyes. She combines, according to Peter Beales in his *Classic Roses*, "…all the best Alba attributes. Blush-pink, it has a refined perfume and is amply clothed with blue-grey leaves." Perfumed? Clothed? Are we talking about plant or woman here? Known from at least the 15th century, Maiden's Blush has a multitude of other aliases, most of them aimed at reading a little too much lasciviousness into her beauty. If you don't like the British name, I could submit it to you as 'La Séduisante', La Virginale', 'Incarnata', or, my favorite, the French name of 'Cuisse de Nymphe' (thigh of the nymphe). I think the translation of the former three aliases is probably evident from their roots. In fact, Mr. Beales relates to us that the name applied to the more richly colored blossoms is 'Cuisse de Nymphe Émue', translated as "thigh of the passionate nymphe." Michael Pollan, in *Second Nature* states that "her petals are more loosely arrayed than Madame Hardy's; less done up, almost unbuttoned. Her petals are larger, too, and they flush with the palest flesh pink toward the center…concealed in the multiplication of her labial folds." Oh Lordy, get a cold shower Michael. One can't miss the anthropomorphic implications, and yet, I don't feel Mr. Pollan is simply standing around ogling the scenery; there is something about this rose which I must agree draws in man and beast, or at least, man. Is it any wonder that I've fallen in lust with this mistress of the rose world?

Choice number acht would be another rarely known Buck rose that I believe deserves much greater recognition and planting. 'Freckles' was a happy accident that I picked up for half price at, believe it or not, one of the seasonal grocery-store garden centers a few years back. The rose was not blooming at the time, but I recognized the name from the tag as likely belonging to one of the Buck roses I had read about and I took a chance that memory served me correctly. And did it ever! Freckles is a hardy, fully-double hybrid tea-like bloomer bearing four to five inch light scarlet blooms singly and in clusters. The blooms are heavily stippled on the inner surfaces of the petals with dark claret rose, hence the name. I've only seen one other rose with similar stippling, the Canadian rose 'Morden Ruby', and both provide a unique conversation piece for the garden. Freckles is also completely disease free in my garden, and blooms continuously from June till frost as an erect bushy shrub. With Freckles, Dr. Griffith Buck bred a winner and bestowed it with a happy name to keep our amusement.

With my ninth choice I will bow to the establishment and choose a modern hybrid tea. Now there, there, don't cry, I haven't abandoned totally all my principles and you knew there had to be at least one. There are a number of hybrid tea roses that I favor that are either marginally hardy ('Helen Traubel') or fully hardy ('Dr. Brownell' or 'Belinda's

Dream') in my garden. I'm also partial to many of the winners of the James Alexander Gamble Fragrance Medal awarded by the American Rose Society to exceptionally fragrant hybrid tea and floribunda roses carrying an ARS rating of over 7.5. These roses include such classics as 'Mister Lincoln', 'Double Delight', 'Sunsprite', and 'Granada'. But, I believe if I had to choose only one hybrid tea rose, it would be the cardinal red 'Olympiad', bred in New Zealand by the great rosarian Sam McGredy. Olympiad is almost cane-hardy in my area, requiring minimal winter protection, and it is blackspot resistant and free-flowering in classic hybrid tea form. It is not exceptionally fragrant, but its bright red color draws me across the garden and it holds its form well as a cut flower indoors. It received the All American Rose Society designation in 1982 and thus grows well throughout the climates of North America.

My tenth and final submission for all-time best rose is a return to both my prairie environment and my ethos. A rose that I would not wish to live without in my garden is the tough as nails cross between *R. spinosissima* and *R. foetida* known as Harison's Yellow. There are many stories of its introduction ranging anywhere from 1824 through 1842 in various sources, but all seem to relate to its origin point as being upstate New York during that period. It then has a fabled distribution of following the pioneer wagons across the United States, leaving pieces of itself at every homestead and perhaps being the shrub known as the mythical Yellow Rose of Texas. The rose is a sulphur-yellow, once-blooming prickly monster of a shrub, keeping the small leaflets of *R. spinosissima* in its form and gaining the bright color and also the unfortunately musky odor of *R. foetida* from that parent. Harison's Yellow blooms early in my garden, right after 'Marie Bugnet' and it then steals the stage with the bright yellow blossoms calling across the garden. Completely hardy into Canada, completely resistant to disease, and containing enough prickles to form an impenetrable barrier to man and beast alike, Harison's Yellow is a rose likely to outlive the gardener and the garden as civilization falls.

Garden Style

I've been for some time perplexed over how to describe to others my personal garden style or garden philosophy. To have the audacity to write about one's garden, one would hope that enough of a style exists for others to recognize it as more than a botanical collection. But in the true self-understanding of an unrequited academic nerd, I'm not disposed to feel that it's likely I show style here in my garden where it is lacking elsewhere in my life. While I think it is a likelihood that my hodgepodge of a garden might have a bit of some type of style, I must confess that I have a tough time defining or categorizing that style at present. It perhaps would be best to approach definition of my garden by what it is not, as if in some alternative universe a positive might be the conclusion from a series of negatives. It is certainly not a formal style garden, neither in the European or Japanese traditions, nor an English border garden, nor is it of the modern xeriscopic or natural gardening styles as might befit my climate at least during the summer months. It is not a Zen garden, botanical garden, kitchen garden, or cottage garden. It is not a woodland, shade, or water garden. It is certainly not a garden designed for the flow and ebb of color by providing drifts or groups of three, five, seven, or nine identical plants together. To put it in the words of Helen Dillon writing to her friend, the gardener Rob Proctor, I, "admit I sometimes plant in drifts of one." It lacks, as a basic definition of a garden, an enclosure of any structure, but instead the background is the grassed hills and overgrown draws of Kansas. It lacks, at this stage in its young life, established paths of more than mowed grass. It lacks the large structures (garden sheds, trellises, large statues etc.) of an established and expensively organized and displayed garden. Structures are something yet to come in my garden, with the laying of brick pavers and walls far in the future awaiting both the discretionary time and money of my older years. It's only current structures are in the random layout of beds edged with limestone, the latter a necessity to keep prairie fires from sweeping the beds, in an occasional bit of statue or bench, and in a just-erected and extremely inexpensive Wisteria trellis near the back border. It lacks a cohesive theme of plant genus, color palettes, and stonework.

I perceive, though, it **is** a garden in that it is organized into beds, with mixed shrubs, grasses and roses, and it does borrow from natural gardening styles and xeriscopic garden vistas. It is also in some areas (the hybrid rose bed), formal in feeling. My garden does have an overriding emphasis on roses. And it is also filled with daylilies and flowering shrubs of various genus, all chosen to grow easily and well within this climate. Is it then, I often have wondered, a collector's garden, or is merely a testament to one gardener's desire to watch life grow under his thumb? While at times, my tendencies for plant collection make it lean towards a botanical display garden (I rarely buy two of the same variety of any given plant species), the overall mix of plants is pleasing and, as previously stated, the colors are, I must say, at worst acceptably arranged. I have an eclectic garden, with a bit of mixed borders here, a shrub rose area there, a "Yellow and Blue" garden, a "Red" garden, a "Spring border", and a "Peony bed". Many of the plants are displayed as individuals, among a backdrop of common perennials, roses interspersed with iris and daylilies, viburnums mixed with grasses, peonies mixed with, well, nothing but peonies.

My search for a description of my garden style came to me finally, this weekend, a humid and balmy typical late June in Kansas, while taking pictures of the front garden beds. My garden is an example of the various stages of a voluptuous or bountiful garden style. In true "cup runneth over" style what I have created at least in the more established front beds, is a merging, flowing, hodgepodge of floriferousness that threatens to engulf the house and sidewalks and expand across the lawn and likely the continent if unchecked. Okay, somewhat an exaggeration, but in an unplanned manner the overwhelming feeling of my front garden, the garden seen by the neighbors, is that of a brazen brothel, brimming with fecundity and teeming with life. Some of that bountifulness is a byproduct of my distaste for trimmed shrubs, and some is because I allow plants to self-seed and select where they're happiest.

Upon further reflection, my garden here is a reflection, like all gardens, of the gardener. It's said that Gertrude Jekyll started a garden movement for borders with drifts of color because her eyesight was so poor she could only see blurred colors and images. And it's said that the hybrid tea form was developed in roses because of the Victorian urge to keep the sex hidden, to keep the flower parts covered and chaste. So it is that my garden reflects my philosophy both in work and in parenting. I've always been of the approach that we can have little effect, in the end, on how our children grow or where they spread. They have their set genetic background and we can only provide a nurturing environment and then it's up to the child to reach for the sun. And with my students, I teach primarily by example and by mentoring, by providing them with resources and by letting their natural abilities and intelligences grow on their own, nudged here and there into a direction which they seem to be inclined to grow, but unpruned, to reach their potential. I hate to spoon feed students, the same as I hate to coddle plants. Each must, after a time, learn to stand on their own. Sometimes, in the garden, I see a plant take off, cast off its immature childhood, and mature into the beauty it was meant for, much like my teenage daughter suddenly transformed last summer from a young filly, all skinny legs and braces, into a beautiful and confident young woman. Isn't it odd how we celebrate the growth of plants, but sometimes are a bit melancholic about the growth of our children?

The Tiller, or Things We Learned From Our Fathers

Like many others of my generation, I had a widespread and long-term gardening education from my parents and grandparents which included lessons on how to start the rototiller in order to cultivate the garden, how to mow the lawn, how to bush-hog the fields, and what a ripe cherry looked like. That education unfortunately didn't include very much about growing ornamental plants if you grew up in Indiana in the 1960's and '70's. And when my own garden gene activated in my early thirties and I first began a vegetable garden, I realized with a shock that I knew the general sequence in which to plant most vegetables, but I had no idea of when or how to actually START. I helped my father plant our garden every year in my childhood, and I knew that the first row of the garden was always onions, followed by rows of peas and lettuce, then potatoes, then sometimes carrots or beets, then tomatoes, and finally at the right hand edge of the garden, sweet corn (crop rotation was not on the agenda). But despite years of experience in planting these vegetables, and although I know the up and down ends of the onion bulb and how deep to plant the lettuce, I didn't know whether to plant onions in January or in May, or how much time should be allowed between planting each different vegetable. I had always considered myself pretty self-sufficient and it was humbling to know that I would've starved to death if I'd suddenly found myself the last man on earth with a bunch of unlabeled seed packets and without instructions. Luckily for most beginning gardeners, printed seed packets and reference books provide that info, and for the scientifically inclined, a good germination chart and a soil thermometer can really maximize your germination and crop survival.

Obviously, Dad was not a believer in the concept of crop rotation, if he had ever heard about it, and in fact, my farming grandfather also never rotated the crops in his vegetable garden either. My grandparent's garden was the same pattern, the rows of onions and potatoes nearest the gate, the corn and squash farthest way. My childhood experiences with crop rotation actually makes me suspicious today when I read about the need to move tomatoes around the garden to prevent disease, since we didn't seem to have many problems in soil where tomatoes had grown for at least thirty years, give or take a foot or so each way. And most of the varieties I plant today are bred to have far more resistance to the very diseases we rotate against. However, following the "experts," and primarily because I learn by reading, I now dutifully move the various plots of my own garden around yearly so that tomatoes or potatoes are never in the same place. Somehow the squash bugs and vine borers are still able to find the zucchini and pumpkins. Right now, in my garden, one of three zucchini plants has succumbed to sudden wilt, despite being planted in a location I've never grown zucchini before and despite spraying toxic pesticides within the last week.

It's always the simple things we forget to consciously state and thus fail to pass on as accumulated wisdom to our sons. I was forty years old before I learned on my own that you didn't have to use all your strength to remove a bit from a socket wrench, but that pushing the square knob on the back releases it. Dad also didn't pass along the importance of placing pre-tension on the starting cord for jump-started tillers and lawn-mowers before pulling the cord. And such a simple thing as pulling that cord tight before you tug on it allows one to start most chainsaws, trimmers, tillers, and mowers with ease. I was given many of these chores at an early age (well, except the chainsaw), and it was seldom that I got a motor started with less than a hundred tugs. I particularly remember battling my nemesis, The Tiller, an unknown brand, unwieldy, unbalanced yet heavy machine built for use while dinosaur dung was still used for manure. Trying to start it should have been labeled as an aerobic training exercise for the Olympics. I still have significant remaining upper body strength in my late forties and I believe I owe that remaining strength to trying to start The Tiller when I was ten. On second thought, The Tiller would have been banned from the Olympics because of the many injuries associated with starting it. Any episode with The Tiller left me either black and blue as it tipped over and fell on me or when I fell on it in exhaustion, deaf from the airplane decibel levels put out by the engine, burnt from falling on the hot motor, or limping from having the tines catch my toes. By the time I got The Tiller started, I was always out of breath and too tired and sore to do any actual tilling. I never had to worry about idling the engine to warm The Tiller up; it was quite warm from all the pulling and also from the warm air accompanying the stream of curse words aimed at the mower and the warmer sweat dripping into the innards. I believe I first learned to curse while starting The Tiller. Once you got it running, The Tiller was guaranteed to die at least four times during a session, necessitating another strenuous start. Sometimes, in the garden, it would hit a subsurface rock and rocket ahead, pulling your arms out of their sockets, and then it would flip over and die. You used your toes to gather up your arms and reattach them and then you lifted The Tiller into an upright position and restarted it, the entire process taking approximately one hour. Even if you successfully kept The Tiller running and got some work done, it was guaranteed to vibrate your hands and arms numb before the second row was tilled. And it delighted in moving sideways in surprise moves, wiping out a significant portion of the sweet corn every chance it was given. I hated The Tiller. Dad still has it, by the way, and it runs just fine, forty years later, proving once again that evil never dies.

Sometimes the lessons we learned from our fathers were, in the best spirit of learning from the mistakes of others, examples of what not to do. And working under my father was a heck of an education in that regard. As he would freely admit, my Dad was neither the most mechanically-oriented father on the block, nor was he obsessive about the condition of his tools. We never fixed anything on our own. If it was motorized, and it didn't make a putt-putt sound, it was sent on its way to town. My grandfather used to bemoan the lack of regular grease and oil given to the farm tractor and Dad was always running the thing into something and banging it up. To be anywhere near Pop when he was bush-hogging was to risk having a lethal missile thrown out of the bushhog at you since he never cared about whether it was vegetable or mineral he was mowing. Most of the other farm implements were never in the best of shape either. I distinctly remember shoveling corn from an ancient flat-bed farm wagon with a broken axle during -20°F weather with a gale blowing. Common hand tools suffered as well. I never knew us to have a hoe or axe that was sharp when we needed it. Dad never got the concept of organizing tools and placing them back into a specific place, at least until after I left home. If you needed a specific wrench, it could usually be found in one of a hundred places after a mere week or so of searching. Most of the time, I'd get blamed because I had moved it from one of the hundred places where Dad knew it was to one of the other ninety-nine places without telling him. I'm sure I never actually lost any tools of his, and the green-handled adjustable wrench of his that's been in my toolbox since I left for college doesn't count. Usually the tools were in the last place they were used, so that helped narrow it down if we could remember where we were when we were using the large Phillips screwdriver the previous summer.

And you could always count on Dad to underestimate the time and amount of work of every project, thus making it easy to start work and hard to finish. Dad had taken to heart the ancient wisdom that the best way to keep a growing boy out of trouble was to put him to good honest labor. As an example, when I was first placed in charge of the cattle at home, Dad decided the barn needed cleaned of manure so we borrowed my grandfather's two-ton manure spreader and he handed me a pitchfork, telling me it might take one or two loads to clean out the barn. Two weeks and thirteen full spreader loads later, the barn was clean and I had learned my lesson. The lesson was that cleaning a barn with a pitchfork is for the Amish, who do it as a lifestyle, not a part-time farmboy. Come to think of it, I've since been in a number of Amish barns where the ceiling is approximately three feet above the manure-covered floor. I demanded we buy a front-end loader for the tractor the following year.

So, as proof that the human race continues to evolve, I currently take exquisite care of my tools, wiping them down with oil every season, placing each into their allotted place, keeping them sharpened, and keeping them under lock and key so my children and wife can't lose them for me. I religiously change the oil in my lawnmower and grease the axles and wash out the mower deck every time I mow. I do send the mower out to be repaired when it doesn't go putt-putt, but I've become pretty handy around the house and can usually fix simple things like faucets and downspouts. And out of experience, I usually triple the time I really think it will take for me to do a project.

I can thank my father, though for a number of positive gifts he passed on. One was the ability to rise early in the morning and get to work. To this day, I enjoy the garden work best in the dawn, when the air is cool, just like Dad did. And the second gift is that I'm one of the lucky few gardeners who are immune to poison ivy. I can pull the stuff out with bare hands without a single blister developing, and I once worked for a week building a fence for Dad in a patch of pure poison ivy and got absolutely no lesions. Oh, wait, my father breaks out at the mere mention of poison ivy. It's my mother who passed on the immunity for it. Anyway, sorry Dad, about the green-handled wrench.

Blue Thoughts

Blue is my favorite color for flowers in the garden, as it is for many other gardeners. For some gardeners, this preference is said to be because of the rarity of blue flowers in nature. After all, we must admit that delphinium blue pigments don't exist in a number of plant genus's including popular favorites such as roses, daylilies, or lilacs. Other gardeners, like Eleanor Perenyi (*Green Thoughts*), write of the mass liking for blue being second only to white as a means to display taste and refinement in the garden. I disagree with Ms. Perenyi. Despite the volumes written of the fabled White Garden at Sissinghurst, for me white just fades in the Kansas sun while blue reflects the Kansas sky.

My personal preference for blue comes not because it's my favorite color overall (I like bright green the most), nor is due to the testosterone surges that occur when a certain female co-worker half my age states, agreeing with my wise and beautiful wife, that she thinks I look best in blue. I really can't explain what it is for me, but if I connect with my feelings (if that's possible in a middle-aged male), I'd say that I feel "soothed" or "rested' by blue in the garden.

I have blue sprinkled throughout my garden in a number of places, but I have concentrated it on the left front of my house, in a bed which I've primarily limited to blues and yellows. In that bed, the blues of bush clematis (*Clematis integrifolia*), and iris (*Iris germanica* 'Full Tide') mix with the yellow of daylilies and oranges of Rudbeckia. Sometimes the blues and yellows of the various flowers even coincide, but, no matter, if they won't bloom simultaneously together, they do in my mind's eye.

I'm always on the lookout for blue flowers whether I'm at a garden shop or just driving through a neighborhood. If you feel the modern bad habits of driving while on a cell phone or driving while doing makeup are dangerous, just follow me down a street in June, when I'm liable at any random time to slow down or come to a complete stop while I ascertain what plant has provided a glimpse of blue beside a house or down an alley.

Worse yet, I am a complete sucker for any plant that is pure sky blue, be it within my hardiness zone or not. I grow great blue flowers such as delphinium and the clematis's 'Romona' or 'The President', irises such as 'Blue Staccato' and 'Full Tide', and the blue balloon flower, all of which are good clear blues with no hint of red or yellow. Among the native wildflowers I allow to pop up wherever they can in the garden is the blue sage (*Salvia azurei*). The perfect light sky-blue, this wildflower is well-behaved in my garden and it likes the dry conditions of the region. I can grow some tolerable blue-tinged flowers such as the lilac 'Wonderblue' until cultivars with better blues come along, and I have some magnificent specimens of daylilies tending towards the purple and blue, albeit with their typical orange tinge or yellow throats. I grow butterfly bushes *(Buddleia davidii)* in vague shades of blue and lilac, and I've developed, by immediately weeding out self-seeded and self-bred plants that don't match up to my color preferences, a wonderful strain of self-seeding columbines that range from light clear blue through true dark blue and into deep violet. I will probably be one of the misguided souls who would buy a sky-blue rose if and when the mad scientists of the genetic plant world get around to making that unnatural creature a reality.

I also grow a number of "blue-foliaged" plants, although I sometimes have trouble seeing the blue shading that gives these plants their name within the overwhelming green of their mass. Blue-leaved hostas, blue-needled conifers, are all fine plants, but I would place them within the marine-blues or greens before I would acknowledge their acceptance into the blue family. The sole exception may be the blue Lyme grass (*Elymus arenarius*), which I find a fine blue tint and use as an accent in my front garden. I'd grow a lot more of it except I discovered early after planting that it will spread like mad and I quickly dug it up, replanted it into buried containers, and thus limited the time it took to eradicate it from my garden to a mere three years. For those who want it, beware, the plant should be sold with a hazard sign and a nurseryman whose sole job it is to grab and shake senseless anyone who gives it the slightest glance while plant shopping.

King of the June Bugs

Along with the evils of corn earworms, I discovered in the fifth year of my garden that I've got to take up arms against yet another pernicious pest. Several years back, as the dwarf peach trees held their first fruits, I noticed that as they ripened, and usually just before I deemed them ready to be plucked from the tree, they developed a curious lesion as if something had crawled up the tree and bit into them. Just a quick nibble mind you, no wholesale removal of the flesh from the pit, no shredding of the skin.

As the peaches affected seemed to be out of the reach of rabbits and deer, and as the accompanying young branches appeared too light for raccoons, and as there are yet no squirrels in my miniature tree'd yard, I concluded that the likely culprits were either birds or the pack rats ubiquitous in my area. I had immediately ruled out insects as a cause as my love for peaches had allowed me to overlook my preference for organic methods and with eyes closed I had been spraying regularly in hopes of a good, if somewhat poisonous, fruit crop. There were occasional similar lesions in the strawberry patch as well and I attributed these to the same creatures or perhaps a box turtle or two, but most times, the injured strawberries were far outnumbered by the juicy whole ones. This went on for a couple of years, a few peaches ready to pick and then ruined on the eve of gustatory enjoyment, a few strawberries nibbled as well. In the interests of interspecies harmony, I agreeably bided my time feeling that eventually the peaches would outnumber the villains and by sheer volume I would at last enjoy the long sought fruits of my labor. Blackberries and grapes, as well, would occasionally disappear, which I again attributed to birds, and my defense against this phenomenon was to cover the bushes and vines with netting, fighting the snags constantly as I uncovered, picked and recovered.

This year however, as the blackberries ripened I got a decent first and second alternate-day picking, but as I went out on the third, I noticed a distinct lack of ripe blackberries. In fact, the whole row of blackberries was stripped of all fruit! Choking back my disappointment, I looked forward next to the peaches, only to see daily that as each peach began to soften it also would acquire the now characteristic bite mark. Mystified, I began checking the trees several times daily, when, finally, at dusk, I beheld the true culprit, clustered around the open wounds in a half dozen peaches. The green June Beetle, *Cotinus nitida*, (also called the June Bug) was the villain, and several were munching away within two days after spraying with permethrin! A quick check of the Internet was sufficient to identify the culprit and confirm its preferences for fresh fruit. Alas, though, the peach season was over. A week later, as I began picking grapes, I again experienced a good first picking but then noticed the grape clusters deflating one by one. Again, checking at dusk, I found clusters of June Bugs, hundreds total on the grape vine. The grape clusters were destroyed. War had been declared and met. It was to be nastier than most.

It should have been obvious but now it was finally clear. In my attempt to satisfy my family's love of fresh fruit, I had planted enough different species that I was continually supplying food for what seemed the entire Kansas population of June Bugs. Indeed, in my harvest rotation of strawberries, raspberries, blackberries, peaches, and grapes, I was providing the perfect Eden for June Bug kind. I had, in fact, unwittingly likely been crowned the King of the June Bugs, or whatever passed for King in the eyes of these demoniac fruitnivores. At least I'm sure they worshiped my every step in the garden if they were capable of perceiving that I was responsible for their current well-being.

Infuriated at the loss of the entire grape harvest, I mixed up a Super-strength solution of several potent and potentially outlawed pesticides and sprayed the beetles, some of whom responded by immediate flight. After my neurologic tremors from the self-absorbed insecticide had subsided however, I noticed a number of the bugs still crawling and munching over the grapes.

Thus, I have opened a second front against this armored adversary, and although aware of the historical fact that opening a second front doomed Hitler and the Reich in WWII, I'm yet optimistic that history will not repeat itself and I will be victorious at the end, perhaps even victorious enough to enjoy an unblemished peach or two on an annual basis. The Internet informs me that the June Bug is a member of the scarab family but even so, this doesn't persuade me to begin considering it sacred in the Egyptian manner. The Internet has unfortunately, however, been decidedly unhelpful in terms of control. It does confirm the nocturnal nature of the pest, and there are numerous sites regarding its control as a turf pest, but not as a fruit chomper. I had high hopes for the site www.Organicgardensite.com which even had a picture of one of the damned beetles on a peach, but its advice was not useful, unless I plan to establish a colony of skunks or armadillos to scavenge the grass for grubs. I've always laughed heartedly at sites that suggest picking the offending insect off by hand. Even if I was willing to touch the things, the sheer number would consume my waking hours for weeks during the summer. A site called "Wayne Schmidt's Gardening page" promotes June bug bashing with a badminton racket, which I believe would be highly mentally and psychically satisfying, but perhaps again, not very time effective and besides, what would the neighbors think to find me flailing about on the prairie in the evening hours and laughing evilly at intervals?.

I'm reduced therefore, to experimentation on the scale of the Manhattan Project. I've currently tried a full-strength insecticidal trap with a peach as bait. Of course, the fiends know of my intention and have not touched the poisoned pome.

I have not yet surrendered, however. Just this week there was a promising article in Fine Gardening about the usefulness of guinea fowl in cleansing the yard of insects. I envision a flock of guinea hens roaming my property will be quite handsome, and I fully intend to employ and exploit the talents of these mercenary soldiers in the near future. The only question here in the Flint Hills is whether the guinea hens will find enough time from running away from coyotes to eat the June bugs. Maybe I can shoot or poison the coyotes to keep them from eating the hens that eat the June bugs who feed at my table. Doesn't anybody else think this is beginning to sound like an Aesop's fable?

Gardening in Burning Hell

Oh whining gardener, why do you complain? Do you fret over the temperature dropping to 28°F or the wind rising to 35mph? Big deal. There is one thing that all gardeners but Kansas Flint Hill gardeners can be thankful for; they don't battle real moving fires on a yearly basis. Well, except for those gardeners in Southern California, but people there just are asking for it when they build their house in the middle of a brush fire pile (the same goes for those who make their homes here in the middle of the prairie and add on a shake roof or wood siding).

Any attempt at a garden here in the middle of the Flint Hills must take into account the annual ritual of burning prairie grass. An astonishingly simple idea, it is nonetheless unfathomable to the modern Americans of the East and Midwest, whose suburbanites have moved onto the former prairies with not the least idea of what created them. There are vast and good texts describing the evolution of the prairies as a result of lightning-sparked grass fires and close grazing by buffalo. To recreate the prairie in my area, one need only burn the dry winter grass, once, twice, and a third time at yearly intervals and soon the native prairie grasses and forbs will emerge again. Cool-season grasses are severely harmed by spring burns, resulting in less competition for the warm-season grasses that make the prairie ecosystem go. Nonnative invaders will be scorched or burned outright. One of the main invaders in our area is the red cedar (*Juniperus virginiana*). Unburned prairies are soon covered with impenetrable groves of this eastern invader. Research on the Konza prairie preserve indicates that the optimum burning interval to maximize the diversity of species on the prairie is about every third year. There are other benefits for ranchers of burning the prairies. Grass on burned prairies has a higher protein level and cow-calf pairs on burned prairie grow faster than unburned pasture. Burning prairies are a springtime right in Kansas, and the burns at night are spectacular as they sweep over the Konza prairie preserve. They are not so spectacular if you care about something in the path of the fire and the fire is out of control.

As an example, after we bought land on the outskirts of town, I began to plan the gardens before I began to plan a house. Since it was January, I thought it'd be nice to start a tulip and daffodil bulb garden to have it ready for spring, and I chose a flat area at the edge of a hillside for clearing. My son, then about eight years old, and I went out to burn a small area, about ten by twenty feet. I wasn't a total fool about it, no not I, the careful farm boy. I knew it'd be hard to stop the burning with the prairie grass a mature three or four feet high. So I picked a completely still, cold January day and took the lawn mower and mowed off the appropriate size patch. We took plenty of water in buckets and in a hand sprayer. We started the fire and I had my son monitor the downside of the hill while I monitored the upside. Then the wind came up. His end of the fire started to get a little bit out of bounds. I went down to help out.

Lesson 1: grass fires on the Kansas prairie move slowly downhill (unless they're driven by a stiff wind), but they move quickly uphill even without wind. The minute I switched downhill to help my son, our fire took off for parts unknown from the upside line. If I had put my end out first, we'd have had all day to put out the bottom side. The minute I knew it was beyond stopping, I called for help. Well, not the very minute because it was in the pre-cell-phone days, and thus I had to drive frantically back to town and call for help. By the time I got back and the fire department arrived, we had a full burn heading for my neighbor's house eighty acres away.

Lesson 2: The volunteer fire department at that time tended to chase fires rather than get ahead of them. This fire was driven by a wind so it had a spearhead aimed due north and they felt they couldn't get ahead of it for fear of losing personnel or equipment (rightfully). I have since learned, though, how often a grass fire can be slowed down dramatically by wetting down the grass even over a narrow area ahead of the running point of the fire. The fire hits the wet line, sputters and slows, and then you have time to put it out. Another important technique is to set backfires to meet runaway fires in areas where you can control the backfires before the heat builds behind them.

Lesson 3: There's no such thing as a controlled burn in Kansas. There are only momentary lapses in uncontrolled burns. I've personally seen controlled burns get away from eight man fire crews with two pumper trucks and a tanker supporting them. I know one guy who swore once at church that the local fire department had started a practice burn on his neighbor's land and it had gotten away from them. As best put by another friend when he accidently burned down his neighbor's pump house, "Another guy asked me if I wanted him to light the grass and I said yes. He asked me if I was sure I wanted him to light it and I said yes. He lit a match, threw it in the grass, and said well, there's no stopping it now. And there wasn't."

The upshot of my own uncontrolled burn was that my little tulip bed fire burned about three hundred acres in a few hours and was stopped just short of the western suburb of town (like at the suburb fence lines). It could have been much worse because to my north is a high area locally known as "Top of the World" and there are a number of houses built there surrounded closely by tall grass. The local firefighters live in fear that a fire will break out in that area and as a consequence they preemptively burn the county parks south of those houses every year to protect them (probably from me). I hate to think what would have happened if the fire jumped the road in that direction. The good news was that the only damage was to a few Scotch pines owned by my neighbor which were scorched on the bottoms. I offered to replace them, but he declined, and that was a wise move because they get scorched about every other year on average anyway. At the time, there wasn't a monetary fine for losing control of a burn and you did not have to get a permit. Both were instituted in our county shortly thereafter.

It only took a couple of years before I realized that if I was ever to have a garden or an orchard, they had to be protected from fires. I had decided initially to garden on both sides of a ravine near the house, figuring it would make a pretty setting. After the roses caught fire for the second year in a row (from my neighbor's fires), I abandoned that idea and opted to move the beds up to the level area behind the house where I could keep the grass cut down around the beds as a fire suppressant. I have since, learning from more bitter experience, edged the beds with large limestone blocks to keep the fire from entering the mulch. When my neighbors burn, I wait till the fire is headed my direction, and then I set backfires to meet the running spearheads. And I wait for the fire with hoses all around and I wet down the entire vegetable garden ahead of time. When we built the house, I had all this in mind, and if you examine my landscaping closely, there is a stone barrier, be it blacktopped driveway, cement patio, or rock wall landscaping, that surrounds the entire perimeter of my brick house. I also mow a fair distance away from the house, taking a lesson from the military handbooks about clear fields for defense. I was proud once when a neighbor's fire got out of control, and I was standing on my land with two local firemen watching the fire burn down below and one of them looked around and said, "Well, this is one house we never have to worry about."

Despite the value of fire in maintaining the prairie, I have resolved never to start a burn, myself, again. Fortunately for my little spot of the prairie, my neighbors are pyromaniacs and they burn yearly while I merely try to protect my property and gardens. I don't call them pyromaniacs lightly. I was once with them after they'd started a burn and it, of course, got out of control and headed to town. As things were calming down and the fire department had it under some control these two guys drove around to the south end of the fire, near town, and came upon a woman walking a dog and looking at the fire. They drove up and the guy on the passenger side hollered "Did you see who started this fire?" When she said "No", he said "Well, if you do, let us know, we're looking for him!"

What The Heck Is That Plant?

Like many other gardeners, I try my best to label my plants or to keep detailed maps of what goes into my perennial beds. I am a miserable failure at it, but I advise you to be diligent in your own efforts. We all know that remembering the name of that 101st perennial in the Hydrangea Bed will be nigh on impossible, but yet for some strange reason, we always expect to, and the only sure alternative is to write it down the minute it goes into the ground with impermeable ink on waterproof paper and then to lock it up in a safe.

I find that I have a pretty good memory for where all my various rose cultivars are placed and I can usually come up with their names at will (except for some understandable confusion between the old garden roses 'La Reine' and 'La Reine Victoria'), but roses after all are fairly distinct in their form, size and color. It's a different ballgame entirely with daylily cultivars. In the first place I've got over one hundred *Hemerocallis* cultivars and most of the ones I have are a vague shade of orange or apricot. And the ones that aren't orange/apricot are generally purple with yellow throats and I have approximately 20 varieties of those. Or they're one of my ten varieties of near-white daylilies such as 'Gentle Shepherd', 'Absolute Zero', 'Chosen One' or 'Ice Carnival' that I don't have a clue of telling apart without DNA testing. In the second place, I've moved most of them over and over as my garden expanded and although I was careful about noting their original location, I was less careful when I moved them, especially on those frantic nights when I was trying to get it done before a period of rain came in or when I was transplanting them as it was actually raining or snowing outside. In my own defense, I always have the best intentions of keeping track of my plantings. I often plant ten to twenty plants at a time and create little maps made on envelopes or scraps of paper of where each one went into the bed. And then I lose the scrap of paper. Or the paper goes through the wash with my pants and is rendered illegible. Or while I'm writing on it during the rainstorm, it crumbles when I'm halfway through noting where the plants are. Sometimes the maps actually survive to make it onto the computer and my only remaining problem is knowing whether that particular 'Creative Art' daylily went to the left of the *Clematis paniculata* or to the right. And then eventually I move the plant and then note its new location on another scrap of paper. All told, considering the chances of losing the map that establishes the identity of a plant each time it's moved, it's a wonder that anything is identifiable in my garden at all.

There are of course, other ways that I lose the plant's name. Sometimes, during transplanting and dividing, I don't know the real name when I move it and I simply write down that I moved the orange daylily from the house front to a particular spot in the Peony bed. Then six months later, when I find the envelope with the information written on it, I find that I wasn't specific enough about the location of exactly which of the six orange daylilies in the front bed that I moved, or that I'm not sure which of the daylilies in the peony bed it now is. Or I know that I planted a *Miscanthus* but lost the tag coming home from the nursery and now I don't know which of the two grasses in front of me is 'Gracillimus' or 'Graziella'.

And there is the problem of plant death and replacement. I've got two beds that are primarily mixed iris and daylily cultivars. When the thirteenth daylily in a row of thirty cultivars dies and I put another one in its place, it's easy to get a little off on the new daylily's exact location in the bed. Daylily cultivars are the worst since many are the same shade of color as their neighbors. Irises are a little easier to keep track of for if I misplace the light blue iris cultivar, at least another similar one is not likely to be close to the same area and I can re-identify it when it blooms. But the result is that I've got two beds containing approximately one hundred and fifty surviving mixed daylilies and irises in, I've planted over three hundred cultivars into those beds to get there, and I rarely have a clue as to what has survived. Or they really trick me by having one variety I thought dead come up next to a newer planting and then I don't know which orange daylily was which. And I'm ignoring entirely the fact that most of my daylilies came through the local Annual Daylily Society sale and thus I'm depending for my 'Gentle Shepherd' to not be 'Absolute Zero' on another gardener who probably has more daylilies and no better sense of what they are than I do. Or, in yet another problem with death in the garden, I've got sixteen different perennial plants noted as occupying the same space in my computer garden maps, most of which died years ago, and I have to carefully go back and observe all each year to see which actually survived to flower this season. And heaven forbid a plant should die someplace that I knew where it was and come up later somewhere else I didn't plant it.

A gardener can rationalize this problem away by concluding that one hundred and fifty mixed iris and daylily cultivars make a nice display and who cares what the individual names are, but that goes against my plant collector nature. I too much enjoy, after hearing another gardener's lament that 'Ice Carnival' hasn't done well this year in their garden, being able to respond that my own 'Ice Carnival' is doing fabulous. It's just not the same if I reply that a few of my near-whites also have done poorly but one of the really large ones was great.

Placing individual name tags into the garden next to each plant as it is planted would be a fabulous solution, but there are several obstacles to this action. The first obstacle is the lack of an inexpensive commercial plant tag that will survive more than a couple of seasons in the Kansas sun. I've noted that the Kansas State University Gardens do a nice job with individually-made bronze plaques costing probably over a hundred dollars each, but those are a little out of my budget. Those little engraved plastic name plates would work for a time, but are also a bit expensive and would crack outside in a couple of years in my climate. Even the little tin garden stakes available at most plant stores don't fit the bill because at a minimum of seventy cents apiece for the label and stake, it would take almost a thousand dollars to label my garden, not to mention that each would have to be relabeled every couple of years as the Kansas sun bleaches out the label. I know one local gardener who writes the name of the plant on a brick and then places it upside down next to the plant, a method that works quite well as long as you don't mind turning over a brick every time you want to know a plant's name. If you leave the brick with the name upright, the name will be bleached off within a season and although I've tried, no paint, ink, or dye I've been able to find will change that simple fact. No, an accurate map of each bed is the best I can do. I, perhaps, could do better if I didn't plant in the summer and work on the maps in the next winter, trying to decipher what was put into the bed from a dirty and ruined piece of notepaper.

Crape Myrtles

Sometimes, trips to the garden stores are fruitless and at others, fortuity strikes and the gardener is elevated to an emotional plane approaching Nirvana in an instant. A couple of years back, I happily participated in one of those happenstances that every gardener dreams of. While spending my day in a not too useful fashion by accompanying my daughter and wife to a soccer function, I of course planned a side trip to a Topeka nursery in search of *Rudbeckia hirta* 'Prairie Sun', which I had seen at the Kansas State University gardens and been on a quest to find for weeks. Although all of my local nurseries either never carried the variety or were out, this nursery had a number of them available, which I was able to find on my own after being directed by the usual hapless sales clerk to Heliopsis "Summer Sun" and after realizing on my own that it would be labeled and placed in this nursery alphabetically among the "coneflowers" rather than the Rudbeckias, since gardeners everywhere are assumed by nursery persons to be ignorant of Latin nomenclature. Mission accomplished, I bought three of the plants which were gangly in that way of overgrown nursery plants in late

85

summer, but which looked like they might possibly survive the first few days. I then drifted on a whim to the local big box hardware store and JACKPOT! A number of crape myrtles, chief among which was a brilliant red variety named 'Centennial Spirit', each standing four foot tall and priced at $9.98, a steal at that size.

Now, all deference to more southernly-borne gardeners, I'm just barely developing a taste for crape myrtles at present. Henry Mitchell, in *One Man's Garden* states that as a shrub it is grossly neglected by gardeners and that it should be planted everywhere. I've read the praises of crape myrtles in various media for years, the rapturous essays on the tall crape trees of Georgia and Tennessee, but I have never experienced them in blooming glory in anything approaching shrub size. You see, the areas in which I've lived have all been labeled Zone 5 and below, so even cold-resistant varieties such as red 'Tonto' (*Lagerstroemia indica*) or lavender 'Zuni' died or froze back to the ground annually if they survived at all. Several years back this area of Kansas was noted as becoming Zone 6, a miraculous achievement equivalent to me moving one hundred and twenty miles south without having to move a single plant (global warming may not be all bad). Suddenly the local nurseries began to carry a few crapes and this past year, they've expanded more so I'd estimate I could have chosen from ten to fifteen varieties.

Introduced in 1747, the Crape Myrtle is native to China and Korea and hardy from Zones 7 to 9. Moist soil and full sun enhance the bloom and ease of culture, although it is noted as being drought resistant after establishment (thankfully for Kansas). The delicate paper-thin petals of all white, pink, red or purple pastel colors give the plant its name, but in areas where it survives as a shrub or tree, the smooth exfoliating bark is noted as one of its best attributes. I've experienced plenty of the former in Kansas, but have not seen the above ground portions of the plant live to exfoliate the bark. There are several varieties (white, pink, and lavender) that have survived for several years grown in front of a greenhouse at the KSU Gardens, but none of them come back from more than 3-4 feet tall even in this protected position.

I've had a 'Tonto' for a couple of years now. It survived two transplanted positions until settling into its permanent home, still freezes back to ground level every winter, but at this date (August as I write) it is blooming happily and is approximately three foot tall in the middle of a mixed shrub bed. A 'Royalty' crape has gone from much-pampered and barely-survived stem to a foot high shrub and is preparing to bloom. Two other dwarf varieties that I've tried in the past two years have succumbed. I'm going to try the 'Centennial' all out on its own and I also purchased a dwarf red variety (unnamed) to try as a container plant that I will allow protection in the garage this winter.

Why Write About Gardening?

Whether one seeks to live a more fulfilling life, or wishes to discover what is really important to us, there is an easy and almost foolproof method to that answer. Simply ask yourself; if you knew you had one month left to live, how would you spend it? Be truthful. Aside from the usual answers about spending time with family and friends and seeking to provide for loved ones, what would you want to do with the short time left?

The answer to that question, for me, was quite surprising but should have been obvious a long time past. I need to write about gardening, about my garden, and to pass down my stories and feelings of this land. Now before false rumors get started, or my parents read this and panic, let me make it perfectly clear that I'm not dying of terminal disease, at least not yet or at least not of one that I'm aware of. But in thinking about the now famous Last Lecture of Randy Pausch and the excellent book of that name, I asked myself that all-important final question. Seriously. For the first time. And suddenly, all those years of feeling like I had a set of stories to tell or be written, but kept putting off as I planned to live forever anyway and that left plenty of time to do it as I got older, that absolutely undeniable compulsion to write took center stage and it was clear it was time to shut off *M*A*S*H* and *Seinfeld* and start writing. I had written a very few small essays and ideas down, some of which are included here, off and on, over a period of two years, but it was the simple fear of not having time to finish that really made me start.

But, then why write this collection of ramblings? Why write about gardening? My professional training is as a small animal veterinary orthopedic surgeon and I've done it for a long time and I'm, with all given modesty, good at it. One might ask, "why not write about the dogs whose legs and joints you've fixed and the clients you've known?" Why not write about being a veterinary student in the late 1970's and early 1980's and about teaching veterinary students today? I have lots of stories of veterinary medicine (as my students can confirm), I have lots of other interests and rarely lack ways to entertain myself, but I find I don't have the craving, the yearning, to write about veterinary medicine or other subjects. The "why" to these questions are a little harder, but stay in the room as I lay back onto the couch and free associate a bit and perhaps things will become clearer.

I garden. I garden as an amateur. I garden for pure enjoyment. I garden because I love to see things grow, to see that first flower open up on a new plant. I garden because there's always something new to experience, something new to learn. My wife would tell you that I garden as an escape from the house. Those who garden with me in Kansas would say that I garden because I have a strong masochistic streak. Martha Smith, author of *Beds I Have Known*, would say that I garden because it's in my genes. I think all of those reasons are correct.

But I dare to write about gardening, I think, because writing in combination with gardening is where I best express creativity, where I can cast off rules and procedures and do it to my plan, or to no plan at all. I love to read and I read a lot of gardening books. In fact, in proper order, I probably like more to read about gardening than I do to actually garden. Certainly the latter holds true in the depth of winter and heat of high summer. The creativity in gardening and the creativity in writing complement and enhance each other, and thus, I am a gardener and I like to read and write about gardens and can't separate the two.

It's different in orthopedic surgery than in gardening. Surgery, in my mind and perhaps in that of most surgeons, is about precision and efficiency, technique and outcome, all developed over years of practice and under the gaze of a learned elder. There are no surprise outcomes in surgery, or there had better not be many, because good outcomes are merely expected and surprises would be mostly bad. My clients don't like to hear about surprises regarding their pet's care. One doesn't decide to repair a broken bone in some shape other than the one it was originally formed in, and one doesn't decide to place a liver …here… rather than there… simply because its color complements that of the spleen better in that location. One follows the books and performs a surgery correctly, in order and calm and with all care, over and over and over. Improvisations are frowned on, not celebrated. After years at the trade and with a single glance at a radiograph, I can predict within minutes how long a surgery will take "on the table" and exactly how I'll repair a given fracture. And while some clients or students perhaps possess personal traits that are interesting or even amusing, if I indeed wrote about those in James Herriot fashion, I might find that I soon might not have clients or surgeries (and hence no money to garden) since clients and veterinary students tend to frown on having their neuroses and obsessions exposed in print. And certainly, as a tenured professor, I have written and will continue to write about veterinary orthopedic surgery in terms of the science, but the purpose of that writing is to communicate to colleagues far and wide and it is also written in a terse and efficient language.

I garden much differently than I practice surgery. My garden is reasonably orderly, but certainly without rigid rules. I allow plants to grow as they wish at times, smothering their neighbors as need be. And I enjoy surprises. I like best that first opening of a flower one has never seen before, or that first glimpse of autumn color in a new shrub.

I find I write about gardening in the same fashion as I garden. Without more than a general plan, without a steady direction, but as the mind and body takes me. In the garden, I plant this rose here, I water that one there, I remember to trim that shrub over yonder, I move a landscaping barrier. On the word processor I move from this rant about color to that story about insects to this thought about the weather. It's the same, you see?

Weather Weary

One of the more difficult things about living in Kansas is that you simply tire of the weather. It's like the difference between marrying so that you have a companion to talk to and divorcing them because they talk all the time. Now I suppose if I lived in California (otherwise known in the red states as the Republic of Kalifornikastan) or in Florida, I'd get bored by the decently mild climates broken only by the rare hurricane or drought. A Caribbean island like Grenada might be even worse with about 360 days a year that are sunny with occasional showers and 75-85°F degrees night and day. Gee, what do I wear today, the beige shorts or the white shorts? And in Minnesota or Canada I'd surely think winter lasts forever. In contrast, gardeners in other areas of the country probably view Kansas as a place where we definitely see the four seasons and where the weather changes often and where weather plays a big factor in what we plant. That's all true. One of the long-term Kansas gags with a ring of truth is that if you don't like the weather, just wait a couple of hours and it'll change.

But it's precisely all that change, broken by long periods of monotony due to drought or cold, that exhaust the Kansas gardener. There's just so much WEATHER that worrying about and preparing for it just tires us out. The weather does change here, day to day, up and down in temperature, from sunny to storms in a minute. Literally, I've been in the process of building fence in a field on a cloudless day and before I can walk (or sprint frantically) to the truck there will be lightning striking within my horizon. I've seen weeks go by without rain when a sixty percent chance of rain was forecast every day and weeks of daily rain with only a ten percent chance forecast on any given day. All that change keeps us covering and uncovering plants, tying up plants or picking up weather-strewn debris, carrying water in drought or moving in cushions from the rain. A good Kansas gardener lives with one hand on the trowel and both eyes on the barometer and thermometer. And we plant based on weather forecasts. I'm always watching the extended forecasts in the summer to decide if I still have time to acclimate a plant before a period of drought or extreme heat comes in and I have to haul water to the plant and shade it from the sun for eternity (or what seems like it during a long hot summer).

I have many issues with Kansas weather, several of which I've referred to in the chapters titled "The Freeze" and "Gardening in Burning Hell", but first and foremost is the fleeting nature of some of our seasons and the drawn-out monotony of others. Yes, Kansas lies in the center of the country and is (mostly) in the Zone 5b area of the current USDA hardiness map. Yes, we do see all four seasons of weather. The difficulty arises in that the seasons are not of equal length. Summer and winter dominate the weather and calendar, while we're lucky to see spring and fall at all. In an average year, winter (or freezing weather) lasts from roughly late October through early April. Particularly in the month of January, there are usually four weeks when we don't venture out into the garden at all for fear of being mistaken the following spring for a new garden statue ("Martha, where did you find that ugly statue of the old man in the rose garden? Oh Gloria, it appeared just about the time that Tom left for that business trip to Florida that he never returned from"). The only gardening done here in January and February is in catalogues and in the gardener's mind. Spring, or what one would describe as spring-like weather with highs in the sixties, lasts approximately two weeks on the average. By early

May, the daily temperatures are in the high 80's to 90's and the plants which didn't make all haste to put down a good root system start to droop every evening. Summer, lasting from May through September, generally has a climax of about thirty straight days of triple-digit temperatures from mid-July to mid-August when, again, one doesn't venture into the garden, this time for fear that one's belly-fat will melt and run into one's shoes. We merely stare out the windows at the brown shriveled grass and sticklike remnants of annuals and pretend that they will all green up when rain and cooler weather finally come. And fall, while delightful, often occurs for about three days where the trees look glorious and then suddenly the fourth morning the trees are bare and the lawn tractor has to be located by probing each pile of leaves with a long stick lest the next day a snowstorm covers it till spring.

Another issue I have with Kansas weather is the extreme violence that can occur, although that is often mitigated by the extremely localized nature of the damage. As I write this, there was an actual tornado in Manhattan, Kansas last night, the first within city limits for almost forty years. About sixty homes were damaged along with a few businesses, but thankfully there was no loss of life in this immediate area. And yet, my house and yard, less than a mile as the crow flies from the extreme damage, didn't have a single leaf down. Last week there was a hailstorm that sent soft-ball sized hail through car windows and metal sheds on the south side of town, yet it was pea-sized and inconsequential in our area on the northwest side. After living here for nineteen years I've yet to personally see a tornado despite constant ill-advised peering from my windows in the midst of countless thunderstorms. I do love and respect the weather trackers in this area who are constantly looking out for us. Sometimes they are more helpful than I know; I once was listening to a storm tracker on the radio and looked out my window to find that the individual was broadcasting from the road directly in front of my house. At least he wasn't talking at the time about a visible tornado. Of course, the weather trackers in this area have become so good that we had about an hour of warning before the tornado yesterday, which takes all the drama out of guessing when it's coming and what direction it's coming from. Last night, despite the radio reports that a half-mile wide tornado was ripping through downtown Manhattan at that very instant, the rain was heavy enough that I couldn't even see the closest perennial bed in my backyard. I suppose the localized nature of such storms is a blessing, but that same proximity is exhibited in the less violent weather patterns as well and thus makes the amount of rain or snow vary greatly from one area of the county to the next. I can't count the number of times that I've stood on my back patio dry as a bone and stared at rain pouring in town or even on the other side of the draw while sunshine is hurting my eyes where I'm standing. When that happens at times of drought, it causes me to let fly some unmannerly words aimed at enticing the storm gods to try and send a little my way.

And yet, most long-term inhabitants of Kansas and Nebraska will tell you that they love thunderstorms and thrive on them. I love the brooding sky as the thunderstorms come in and I even admire the dark wall clouds when the wind comes up and feeds them. When we first moved to Manhattan my son was a toddler and we'd sit in the nursery and rock him to comfort him while he shouted "Tunder boom, Itening NO!" at every bolt. Thunderstorms in this area can be beautiful and enjoyable when you're indoors and protected from them, and terrifying if you're out in the open. These days, I usually sleep the soundest during thunderstorms, generally falling into a complete relaxation and smiling satisfaction as the rain starts hitting the skylights or sides of the house. Of course that's probably because, however brief, I know afterwards there will be a cooler day and a day of respite from hauling water to new plants.

Sound In The Garden

Regarding gardening in general, a multitude of books exist to aid the gardener in the pursuit of adding fragrance to the garden, or in mixing colors in the garden, or in mixing form, or leaf texture, or light. To my knowledge, however, one area which has sorely missed close scrutiny except in short excerpts would be the treatment of sound in the garden. Now take notice, I'm not referring to the wholesale broadcast of classical elevator music that one finds in some formal gardens. Such a recorded symphonic background is often played at either faintest whisper or at aircraft engine decibels to give one the impression that, well, that one is in a cultured place and that by being there, one is cultured or at least should act cultured. If one needs to think "Ah, Bach" in order to enjoy the beauty and serenity offered by a well-mastered garden, then I believe we've missed the point. I'm of the opinion that proper sounds to accompany a garden are those induced from the garden itself, that a sense of silence and quiet is first and most important. Other natural sounds for a garden include the faint rambling and gurgling of a fountain or stream of water, the whisper of grasses in the wind or the song of a good quail singing "Bob White, Bob White" over and over at 5:00 a.m. until your hands ache for a shotgun. Well, maybe not the latter, but a good dependable warbler can beat Bach any day of the week.

Let me provide a perfect example of where nature's sound triumphs man. To my ears, no sound is more pleasant than the rustling of the leaves of the American Cottonwood *(Populus deltoides)*. I know that most gardening authorities tell us that the cottonwood is a base` tree, soft and prone to breakage, dirty with its million's of downy coated seeds and small twigs that fall incessantly. Yes, yes, I know all that, but I don't understand the tendency to overlook the wonderful form, fast growth, and above all, the shear heavenly sound of this prairie stalwart. I've got them purposely planted in a couple of sites and oh, the chorus I reap! I was reminded this morning as I stepped out to get the Sunday paper. It is a cool, overcast, damp morning, unusual for Kansas anytime except in the spring, and the breeze blowing is so gentle that it could barely be felt, yet the background harmony to the intermittent morning call of the Eastern Meadowlark across the road was the quiet clicking and whispering of the cottonwood forty feet away, a song I love above all other. I'm not sure how closely the sounds from poplar family members which frequent the Rockies resemble the lone cottonwood here in Kansas, but the cottonwood is a sound I would not garden without. I have two larger specimens in my immediate yard; one, a hybridized cotton-less cottonwood, the other a wild form like that pops up here in every ditch where water stands in the spring. My wild cottonwood came volunteer next to my stone landscaping and after chopping it down twice, I finally acquiesced to its life force and transplanted it where it would grow fast and strong. It is now, six years later, the tallest tree in my surroundings and it thanks me for recognizing its right to live with every breeze in the garden. The hybridized variety provides the same song near my bedroom window, but is generally a weaker fellow in growth and form. Yet another example of hybridization creating an inferior copy, but at least the sound is the same. Anyone who voices rapture over a bubbling brook should have a cottonwood nearby to enhance the joy. And to those who listen to the snooty authorities about the common qualities of this tree I provide a second enticement; the fall color is a glorious pure yellow to offset the reds of maple and browns of oak in my yard. And for the patriotic, just look at the old Latin name; Populus americanus; in America, one of the people.

The sound of bees buzzing around the garden provides another calming and natural backdrop to the visual impact of a garden. There is nothing more unobtrusive, or more calming, then the work of bees near either a bed of lavender or a flowering cotoneaster. We have a pair of cranberry cotoneaster (*Cotoneaster apiculatus*) in a raised landscape bed next to the basement door and walking into its vicinity during bloom is like walking into a symphony of industriousness. Another area where the bees rise to notice is on the west side of the house where we have placed a number of lavender cultivars and nearby have a False Spirea (*Caryopteris sp. 'Blue Mist'*). When the lavender and Caryopteris are in bloom simultaneously, the bees react and speed to the area in mass, working a frenzied line between the two areas and one dare not step out into that traffic. But the buzzword in the area is nectar and the workmanlike bees are after it with gusto.

I recently saw a delightful garden on a very windy day on the Junction City garden tour, and this particular garden featured in one area a beautiful cottage garden framed by a classic Kansas limestone barn as the backdrop. The plants were placed into small beds edged with planks and with narrow gravel walkways around each bed and the whole garden was surrounded by a split rail fence. The garden was all in all a very quaint and moving picture. But a key feature of the garden was an old, rusty and large metal windmill, such as is used in the countryside here for pumping water, smack dab in the middle of this garden. There was no pump line attached to the windmill but the old girl turned with a delightful squeaking sound as the frenzied Kansas wind took it to and fro. Now, you might ask why a rusty screech here and there at random intervals would be enjoyable, rather than maddening, but in a way I can't adequately explain, this sound said "I'm here, in the barnyard, and you can count on me to draw the water and ease your work, and you can count on me to sound the alarm if the wind picks up." Every prairie garden should have an identical windmill already or have one added immediately. Alas, my garden does not have a windmill of the large or rusty type, not yet at least, but I have had for several years one of those eight foot ornamental windmills you can purchase at any given farm store. And because I am a bit of a fanatic about keeping things painted, it hasn't yet either rusted or developed a squeak so it doesn't add to the auditory pleasures in the garden. But is does provide similar visual warnings to alert us to the weather in the garden. Pointing south, it tells of a warm wind coming to improve the temperatures (or to make them overhot in the dead of summer). Pointing west, it tells me it's feeding a storm that will soon sweep in and bring the threat of lightening and tornados. Pointing north, it tells of the onslaught of winter as it greets the cold Canadian air masses. And pointing east...well, it almost never points east as the prevailing winds just don't go east to west here.

Of course, most often when an expert gardener or landscape designer thinks of sound in the garden they are thinking of a water feature. Man-made ponds or pond-less water features in the garden are all the rage at the present, here in Kansas and elsewhere, I suppose, throughout the world. I admit that when I have time to visit one of these gardens and sit and listen to the bubbling of a fountain or brook, they are quite soothing and they also bring a cool calm to the area which is refreshing in the humid Kansas climate. I have a friend with a massive pond filled with an ocean's worth of koi, and know another gardener with the good fortune to have a drainage channel cutting through their woodland garden which often has running water. And I know lots of gardeners with small self-installed artificial ponds bubbling near their front or back doors. But none of these are for me. I don't have a water feature in my garden and to the chagrin of my wife, She Who Feels The Pressures Of Society to which I seem to be immune, I don't plan to add one. I've tried a small self-contained fountain or two. But there's something vaguely unnatural and even unwholesome about a bubbling fountain sited with the prairie as a backdrop or even worse, a pond clinging to the side of or perched on top of one of the rolling ridges of this area. We're so attuned to the aquifer levels in Kansas, we're so mindful of the lack of water here in the summer heat, that I'd feel sinful if I were to add a water feature to my garden. I'd feel like Al Gore was jumping on his private plane, on his way to castigate me for wasting precious natural resources that should be saved for the children. I'd feel out of place, like I do in the upstairs bathroom at home, the one decorated by my wife with fish and ocean accoutrements, despite my pleas to remember we live in Kansas, not Tampa. But that's me, a fish out of water.

Bird Treasures

Like many gardeners, I find the local avian fauna to be one of the best entertainments in my garden. I am not one of those delusional souls who garden merely to see how many birds they can bring into their garden, but I do enjoy those birds who themselves enjoy living and eating here. To a certain extent, anyway.

In the early days of my garden, I was suspicious about enticing birds into my garden out of fear that whatever enjoyment I might gain from their presence would be offset by the loss of fruit harvested by me. And as my early strawberry, grape, and peach crops were masterfully being harvested by something other than my family, I felt justified in keeping them at arm's length (even though my ravenous nemesis turned out to be June Bugs). I resorted at one time to covering strawberries and blackberries with plastic net to deter avian invaders, but caught little except a snake whose reptilian demise in the net before I found it invoked a curious feeling of guilt given my usual dislike of things of the slithering family. If I did anything to draw birds in as a general concept, it was to select plants with an eye towards bird-edible fall fruit such as viburnums and choke-cherries and lots of grasses. If you have the same reservations about drawing birds to your garden, cast them aside on my experience. For proof of how little fruit backyard birds eat, this year the dwarf cherry tree (*Prunus cerasus* 'North Star') off my back porch had a fair amount of fruit left on it once we'd eaten our fill, and there are still lots of dark overripe cherries available two months later.

In my prairie garden, I grew first to love the Eastern Bluebird (*Sialis sialis*). This native Kansas bird adds a brilliant spot of moving blue color when present in the landscape; that irresistible (to me) sky-blue shade that I try to add to my garden whenever and wherever I can find it. And it has a number of other redeeming qualities, not the least of which is that its primary food are the insects I would most like to remove from my garden, including grasshoppers. Bluebirds have an endearing method of flight as well, never flying in a level straight line, but flying in "hops" from one spot to the next. Watching one fly always brings a smile to my face. And, in Kansas, it's one of the earliest migrant returns, often beginning nests in available cavities as early as February when the north wind is still howling down the hillsides.

And so I resolved to bring more bluebirds into my landscape and for those with a similar desire, the easiest way is to provide nesting boxes. The Eastern Bluebird is a cavity nester and as old trees with rotten cavities are fewer and fewer in the prairie states, the Bluebird has likewise been in decline in recent decades due primarily to that destruction of its nesting sites. There are entire books written on bluebird nest construction, discussing details in dimensions, entry hole diameter, and placement, which I won't go into here, but the most important aspect is to place the boxes some distance apart. Thus, there are twelve bluebird boxes placed over the twenty acres of home, with one box being only peripherally within view of the next, but all with a wide view of the prairie. I'm pleased to report to the environmental wackos that I'm doing my part in the bluebird renaissance, with my record being eight bluebird nests in the twelve boxes in a given year.

A similar but contrasting spot of color to the bluebird in the garden is the bright yellow American Goldfinch (*Carduelis tristis*). It is found throughout the year in my area, although I've noted that it becomes visually scarce in summer and gathers around my feeders more in spring and fall. Above all else, to draw in the goldfinch means that one must provide either thistles or thistle seed, and since I'm not fond of mass plantings of thistle in my landscape, I opt to artificially bring in the goldfinch with cash-purchased thistle seed. Man's ingenuity shows in the production of thistle feeders these days, as feeders designed to thwart sparrows and others take advantage of the fact that the goldfinch is the only bird in this area that can take seed from a feeder while hanging upside down.

I've also become rather fond of my Purple Martins (*Progne subis*), for many of the same reasons as the bluebirds. If you haven't yet experienced it, setting up a purple martin house really has nothing to do with the mythical number of mosquitoes and gnats these aviators will consume for you, but it has everything to do with helping you overcome the boredom of mowing the lawn. Mowing my lawn with the purple martins is like watching a choreographed Russian ballet for hours on end, with the martins ceaselessly swooping around the moving lawnmower in search of the insects it disturbs. As they dart first this way and that, I've at times been afraid of catching one smack in the face, but so far, the martins have managed to avoid such distasteful collisions and pull gracefully away at the last minute every time. Like the bluebirds, the martins are fastidious about their nesting requirements, but once satisfied in a perch high above the prairie and within sight of a pond, they will return year after year to keep the dances coming.

This summer, a different sort of entertainment was provided to me by a protective female Common Nighthawk (*Chordeiles minor).* In the cypress mulch around a young Walnut tree, this goatsucker laid eggs and hatched two fledglings who survived to adulthood under my weekly watchful eye as I mowed. Those of urban uptight background might think that laying eggs on the bare ground hardly qualifies one for exemplary motherhood, but this Nighthawk was exceptionally canny in her selection of the nesting area as the mulch provided the perfect camouflage to her brown and tan wing patterns and those of her chicks. If you looked closely, you would recognize that cypress mulch does not have perfectly round dark black eyes, but that was sometimes the only indication of their presence. And protective this mother goatsucker was. As I mowed near her chicks, she would suddenly dart from invisibility to flight, landing ten to fifteen yards away and trailing a wing as if crippled to entice me (the roaring predator with the whirling blades) to follow her away from the nest for an easy kill. This went on for several weeks, my mowing close, and her feigning sacrifice for her chicks, but the chicks themselves, as they grew, rarely moved no matter how close the lawnmower got. Somehow, they knew that their survival depended on their invisibility, and that movement would only focus attention upon them. Well, okay, as they got a bit larger they would sometimes sneak off into the grass as I approached with the lawnmower and I spent several anxious weeks peering closely and moving slowly less a sudden "whompf" and spray of feathers ruin my mowing experience. But the chicks just got bigger and bigger under mama's watchful dark eyes until one day, they were just gone.

None of those previously mentioned though, elicit for me the calm knowledge of feeling at home on the prairie like the Northern Bobwhite (*Colinus virginianus*). If I've got a bobwhite pair in my shrubbery each summer, I know that my home is inviting to others and comfortable to visitors. The bobwhite is often invisible here, sometimes recognized as being present only by the musical "Bob White" of its call, but often, walking through the prairie grass, or near my landscaped beds, I find myself following one or two quail as they dart from bush to bush, grass clump to cover, always staying slightly ahead, but never seeming to panic as their little legs churn across the grass. Get too close, though, and they'll explode in quick low flight to safety.

I have always taken pleasure in the ways of quail, for they are the most exemplary moral citizens of my landscape. They seem to be monogamous to a fault, with the result that each year I name a local pair as "Bob and Judy" Bobwhite, but of course for all I know they swap spouses every season as winter cabin fever causes them to tire of the old. They take up residence for a summer, often quite close to the house, beneath a bush or in a clump of grass, and can be reliably found there despite the occasional encroachment by hunting house cats and nosy dogs. If you feed them natural grain or cracked corn, they will come to your bidding as reliably as a faithful horse and each has its own personality and mannerisms to distinguish it. This one grabs its food and carries it off a few paces to eat with its back turned. That one gobbles from step to step, hurrying through its meal in case the cats are set free upon them. My neighbor feeds them regularly, but his motive, being a hunter, is motivated from love of plump flesh rather than love of mannerism. To me, their little plump bodies make them cute to a fault, irresistible in the way that babies are irresistible. My life would be less complete without my yearly quail friends.

The Truth about Low-Maintenance Gardens

There exist many complete garden books and an infinite number of garden columns in magazines that are devoted to the creation of the low-maintenance garden. All these and more are filled with timely advice and bits of wisdom. Older books like *How to Have a Green Thumb Without an Aching Back* by Ruth Stout and newer books such as *Weedless Gardening* by Lee Reich are excellent to show us how to use mulch to decrease our weeding chores. Experts on arid gardens shower us with information on how to create a water-wise garden and decrease the time we spend watering. Many books are written on time-saving and labor-saving methods such as on layering materials for on-site composting (*Lasagna Gardening* by Patricia Lanza), mulching with permanent materials in xeriscapes (*Beth Chatto's Gravel Garden* by Beth Chatto), and on other low maintenance methods (for example, *The 5-Minute Gardener: How to Plan, Create, and Sustain a Low-Maintenance Garden* by Brenda Little). In fact, hundreds of texts are out there waiting to persuade us that this author or this gardener has the solution to all our troubles.

Garden Musings

This spring, it occurred to me that I have actually attained the often-sought-but-seldom-reached goal of a low maintenance garden. The utopia of gardeners everywhere is within my grasp. My epiphany appeared in a moment of quiet exhilaration when I realized that with about four days work I had reached the point of "spring cleanup and major projects complete." That was even including cleaning up from last December's disastrous ice storm which by itself added a day of trimming trees and pruning roses to my usual spring chores. I had the fall and winter debris removed, the roses trimmed, the main beds weeded and mulched, the fertilizing done, the hoses out, the electric fence in the vegetable garden repaired, and I'd burned the pastures. Additionally, I had a burst of energy and had placed out a skid of landscaping rock that had sat in place for two years, cleaned up two piles of flint rock chips that had accumulated about five years ago when clearing the lawn, moved or divided about sixty plants, picked up a couple of rock piles, and built a wisteria trellis.

I am most happy to take full credit for my break-through in low-maintenance, but I also feel compelled to unburden my conscience. Consciences, in my experience, are often a nuisance, not unlike cats calling for their evening tuna. In that vein of full disclosure, my practice of low-maintenance stems not from any expertise in the subject, nor from careful study of garden books or experimentation with gardening methods. My low-maintenance garden was created and exists solely as an expression of my innate laziness.

This confession comes (I hope) as a surprise to those who know me because I believe I'm mostly known to those other than my wife as an industrious fellow and the sole dissenter is jaundiced by my efficient procrastination on "honey-do" projects. It's true, given a choice between planting seeds and changing the recessed light bulbs in the den, I usually choose to feel my way around the dark for a few weeks before addressing the latter. I commonly have a lot of garden and other projects dancing in the wind and can get quite a bit accomplished in a short time, but my main motivation is to avoid work at all costs, even if avoiding work requires slightly more effort than the work itself would have involved. The standing joke in my family as I was growing up was that my pattern was to read and read and read before I did something new; to read so much about what I was going to do that I was an expert before I did it. Little did they know it was just another manifestation of laziness; I read about things so that I did them right the first time.

As an example, my vegetable garden is completely mulched with thick layers of straw. Yes, I have read Ruth Stout's *The Ruth Stout No-Work Garden Book* and Patricia Lanza's *Lasagna Gardening*. I understand the seemingly miraculous advantages of the thick permanent mulches for soil productivity, moisture conservation, and earthworm ranching. I was raised a Methodist, though. Methodists by nature and nurture don't generally get into evangelism very quickly or fervently, whether one is talking about religious movements or organic gardening movements. And if there's one point I think everyone would agree with, it's that organic converts seem to become a bit fanatical, or dare I say "strident" in their support for their new found devotions. In fact, movies depicting the activities of Hitler or Communist Party Youth pale in comparison to the actual actions of the average organic garden devotee. So however organic and environmentally beneficial it may be, the permanent mulch approach for me is advantageous because I don't have to till the soil and I don't have to pull weeds. I have in fact been known, from time to time, to walk through the vegetable garden with a sprayer of diluted Roundup, on the simple theory that it's easier to zap the weeds that make it through the mulch with herbicide than to bend over and pluck them individually. And please, don't lecture me about toxic herbicides and environmentalism. I'm a scientist, I know good science, and Roundup is less toxic than rainwater (at least given the acid rains seen in the northeastern US these days).

My garden is also low-maintenance because I simply don't or won't perform many of the tasks that others consider essential for a good garden but which I just look on as work. For example consider the act of deadheading. I don't deadhead. I don't understand why anyone would want to flip around their garden every day cutting off dying flowers in an effort to keep it tidied up or to promote a little more bloom. I do love plants that spontaneously shed their spent flowers, thus saving me from guilt over not dead-heading. I enjoy brown seed heads and plump orange rose hips and all the other drying remnants of summer sex in the garden, and I particularly enjoy the sculptures these make when covered with a good ice storm or blanket of snow. I don't feel the need, despite my German heritage and to the chagrin of my father, to have a garden perfectly "in ordnung." I don't want a garden where all flowers bloom continuously either. One of the surprises I've enjoyed about my garden this year is that it is more like viewing a series of musical notes than about watching a symphony. My genus/species tend to be clumped here and there, so one week it may be the lilacs blooming in the bed bordering the garage, the next the peonies in the peony bed, and then later the daylilies bloom in another area of the garden. If I want to extend their blooms I look for different varieties of a given perennial that bloom earlier or later. If I wanted continuous bloom I'd plant annuals in a carpet bed and then start afresh each season.

Pruning is another common garden chore that I tend to avoid like piles of fresh dog feces. To be quite frank about it, I believe that those who force their will on the shape of plants are control freaks that are merely setting themselves up for a big fall when nature intervenes in their plans; either that or they have some deep compulsive disorder that dictates their need to impose their will on their plants. Most woody shrubs in common garden use are more comely, in my opinion, when they are allowed to find their natural form and size. Besides, keeping these plants from their destiny is a little like holding back the tides. They just fight you at every step and increase your workload by their nature. I never touch my viburnums, forsythia, woody hydrangeas, sweetspires, or boxwoods. Is there anything more natural in a garden than the perfect pyramidal lines of a dwarf blue spruce (*Picea glauca* 'Conica'), however commonly planted it may be? Many forsythia, such as *Forsythia X intermedia* 'New Hampshire Gold', make the most perfect masses of arched branches if not arbitrarily clipped into formal hedges. Other cultivars, such as 'Meadowlark', have stiffer backbones and more angled branching, but if left untouched, will leave their own impact on the landscape. In fact my 'Meadlowlark' this year has surprised me by flowering twice, once in the spring and again in August. I will admit to occasionally trying to prune horizontal branches on my foundation hollies so I can get past them to the faucet, but that's the entire extent of my pruning beyond adhering to the 3 D's of removing diseased, damaged, or dead material.

I've never understood or appreciated the art of topiary either. Just last week, I watched an episode of *The Gardener's Diary* on HGTV where Erica Glasener interviewed a South Carolina man named Pearl

Fryar whose entire garden is filled with evergreen topiary and nothing but topiary. Shades of Edward Scissorhands! I've always been a little envious of the ability to create spirals in evergreens and I was quite impressed by the segment in the aforementioned show where Mr. Fryar demonstrates to Erica how to shape a spiraled shrub with a chain saw in approximately two minutes flat. But come on, please, let's discuss obsessive-compulsive gardening, shall we? Though impressed, I have no urge to follow that lead, even though it involves chain saws and horticultural mayhem as enticement factors. Imagine the time and effort needed to maintain formal shapes in hundreds of plants season after season. Formal garden styles are definitely not my thing, primarily because they take lots of effort to maintain.

Double digging? It is to laugh. Another HGTV episode this week, of *Gardening by the Yard* with Paul James "The Gardener Guy" had an episode illustrating the proper method of double digging. Both Paul James and the gardening director for that particular garden spent the time watching a very fit, tanned and buff young man double dig an approximately eight foot by four foot plot of perfect loose soil. The most effort either observer exerted was commenting on how easy it is and how important for soil care. I watched the entire episode and didn't see a single rock or clod in the soil being moved. The soil was as finely textured as if cake flour was being moved. Double digging the same plot in Kansas would have required a bulldozer and six men, not to mention the five ton truck to haul off the rock and clay from the hole. Needless to say, I haven't double dug a single patch in Kansas. Life is too short and the clay is too hard. Yet I still find my asparagus patch is thriving despite the fact that the roots were planted six inches deep in native soil instead of being planted a foot deep in soil that had been worked and amended to a depth of three feet as recommended by many experts. I still find that trees and shrubs do well in my garden even if their planting holes are only ¼ inch larger than their container rather than the recommended "twice as wide and as exactly deep as the root ball." I think there is something to be said for the idea of making the plant's roots extend into regular soil rather than artificially soft or amended soil. But the key to human contentness is our ability to rationalize every behavior we can.

Where the Wind Goes Sweeping Down the Plains

I was looking out the window this morning, shortly after rising, and I said to my wife "Honey, there's almost no wind out there this morning." Her response was "Wow, that's really weird." And it is. We had the same feeling recently when visiting New York City. Something just felt wrong, and after awhile, we both realized we missed the sound of the wind.

The wind in the Flint Hills of Kansas is a constant companion that we really don't notice until it's either not there or it's blowing the trees over on the house. The average annual wind speed for our Flint Hills area is just slightly over ten miles/hour, about the same as Chicago, the so-called Windy City, but it seems like it's normally a lot faster. It's a comforting refrain to listen to the wind howling outside the windows at night. Native Kansans take that as a sign that all is right with the world. Even when it calms down, there's still enough wind to cause the leaves on the native Cottonwood trees to rustle and that provides my favorite music in the garden.

It's actually astonishing how much more wind there is out on the prairie, a mile outside the river valley Manhattan Kansas is placed in, then I noticed when I lived in town. Something about the slight drop in elevation and all the other houses makes the wind in town less omnipresent. On the prairie, every structure we put up, and every plant in the garden needs to be either resistant to the wind, bend with it, or be protected from it. I've given up completely at placing small hoop-formed plastic cold frames over my vegetable gardens because their average lifespan when I tried them was no more than four days before they were ripped to shreds. Because the wind annually has periods where it reaches seventy mile per hour straight line winds, few plants are completely resistant to the wind else they snap off, so that's not a good survival strategy for my plants. Since I don't have a wall around my garden, protection is not an option. So for the most part, plants in my garden must bend to the wind. Tree's in my garden mostly lean a little to the north. It doesn't bother you because you're usually leaning in that direction as well on windy days. Trees here also have a thicker trunk compared to trees in other states.

I learned long ago not to fight the wind. At first, I was constantly distressed when the spring wind would break off a new rose cane before it could flower. Hybrid Teas, always prone to weak constitutions compared to other rose classes, were the worst. But one adapts or else one becomes extinct. I notice that I'm far more fond of landscape grasses than I used to be, and indeed, grasses are fast becoming more popular in the landscapes across Kansas and the Plains. In fact, I've grown to love grasses to the point where I can wax ecstatic about their motions in the wind. I have developed a habit of pinching off the growing ends of new rose canes before they top three feet to limit the leverage on the base of the cane. I prefer to plant deciduous trees such as Cottonwoods and Birch, both of which have less dense leaf masses and don't block wind so much as they pass wind through them. I grow lots of perennials like daylilies and Rudbeckia who are supple enough to bend with the wind.

Far from being a disadvantage, the wind here becomes an ally in creating beauty in the garden. There is something that just feels right about watching tall clumps of *Miscanthus sinensis* sway in the wind. About any variety will work the same. I have 'Karl Foester' 'Morning Light,' 'Gracillimus' and a number of other Miscanthus, and I also find the tall switchgrass *Panicum virgatum* 'Northwind' shows itself really well in the winds.

Kansas, in fact, is rated third in the nation for the potential to provide wind energy exports. I, for one, have no concept of why various groups fight the creation of wind energy farms here in Kansas, but it seems to have many opponents. Some feel that the wind turbines are unsightly blots on the horizons. To each their own, but after passing a large and growing wind farm west of Salina, I can only tell you that I think they add beauty as well as utility to the landscape. In a classic case of split personality, lots of local wild-eyed environmentalists here oppose wind energy due to potential impacts on bird populations, but the Sierra Club and National Audubon society are both in favor of using wind for production of energy over fossil fuels. Looking at the commercial wind turbines, I can tell you that any bird dumb enough to fly into one probably needs a Darwinian adjustment anyway. It isn't like these things run as fast as house fans. And they're a source of needed income to the local ranchers and don't even affect ranch operations to any great degree; cattle graze peacefully around them. A couple of years back, two eastern university professors started a firestorm with their suggestion that western Kansas and eastern Colorado should be turned into a large buffalo commons in order to best match the land with its use. I disagree. I think the land would best be used if it became a large mixed buffalo commons and wind energy range.

Favorite Tools

In the midst of the hustle and bustle of gardening, I have often wished for a good guide for what tools are absolutely essential for gardening. It seems like the media gardening "experts" are all becoming commercially sponsored just like athletes, and they're all pushers for their favorite product lines these days. Soon, I'm sure we'll be able to get a box of Wheaties with P. Allen Smith or Rebecca Kolls gracing the cover. Until then, I guess it's up to me to provide the needed info to my fellow gardeners. At least until somebody offers me a signing bonus to promote Fertilome.

I have a number of gardening tools, but I also have a minimalist nature. So I tend to gravitate only to a group of tools I use comfortably and continually. And the good news here is that it's not expensive to outfit a gardener's tool shed, not really. You just need to keep paring down the stuff you never use. If I buy it and it breaks, I don't replace it. If I buy it and I don't use it, eventually I purposefully break it so it doesn't fall off the rack and smack me when I open the cabinet door. A word to the wise here; do not donate the tools you don't use to

Goodwill or the Salvation Army as an attempt to skimp the federal government out of your tax money. I agree with the motive (keeping the federal government from getting its hands on any more of your income then it can discover), but inflicting your less-than-helpful tools on unsuspecting indigenous victims is just not good Karma.

Let's take pruning tools as an example. Essentially, all my pruning is done these days with four pruning tools. A good pair of bypass hand pruners is a must have, especially for someone with as many roses as grace my landscape. Forget purchasing any anvil pruners of any size and type unless you are have a sadistic streak and imagine plants screaming as you crush their stems. I don't, and so I live by the motto that a good pair of bypass pruners, well-maintained and sharpened occasionally, is like a quick amputation was to people of prior centuries; merciful. And like Porsche as it relates to cars, there is no substitute for Felco pruners. Skip all the fancy crap like rotating handles, a Felco Model 2 (the original) is what you want, whether you're right-handed or left-handed. Yes, I know there are special models for lefties like myself, and more ergonomic models, and models with fiberglass handles but I never had problems using right-handed instruments (and remember, by trade I'm a surgeon), and the greater availability of replacement blades and repairs for right-handed Model 2 pruners means you should learn to adapt. I bought my first pair of Felcos over ten years ago, threw out all the others, and have still never needed to do more than take an occasional file to the edge.

Beyond hand trimmers, you need a well-made large bypass lopper with long wooden or fiberglass handles for larger twigs, a sharp pruning saw for larger limbs, and lastly, if you are the type that thinks topiary is the bee's knees, you need a set of hand-operated hedge shears of good quality. Notice that I've shied away from electric shears and trimmers, whose primary purpose is either to cut their own card and electrocute the gardener or to keep running after the ladder falls and sever whatever limbs (bushes or humans) they come in contact with on the way to the ground.

There must be forty million types of hoes available in the world today, but after trying 35 million of them, I find I use only two; a Warren hoe (or planting hoe) for planting, and a cavex hoe for weeding. The planting hoe is perfect for making all the straight line furrows I need in the spring for planting rows and then covering the seed. You place it down into the soil and pull it towards you, making the furrow. The sharp curvilinear blade of the cavex hoe is perfect for running at the soil surface and cutting off weeds. In the Kansas soil, you can forget about the Dutch or scuffling type hoes which serve merely to shock your arms as they scrape over the chert pieces in the soils, and you can also forget about the ubiquitous "garden hoe" sold everywhere as the latter is primarily made for chopping and weeding in light sandy soils that are found only near seaside beaches or the middle east.

To plant, you need not a shovel, but a good grade steel spade, sharpened at the leading edge so that it penetrates the soil easily. It also helps to have a spiritual guide to learn how to properly use the spade as it took me several years to realize they weren't made for hopping onto with both feet simultaneously. And, okay, I admit that I prefer a small shovel with a long handle for planting bulbs and garden plants rather than a hand trowel or dedicated bulb planter. I own several trowels, but use none of them; too much arm work when your legs can do the digging. And as far as bending over to place the bulbs, what else are children for?

Let's see, what else do you think you need to garden? I think a good hand sprayer of approximately the two gallon size is a must for my garden for the spraying of various poisons if one cares to harvest edible fruit or vegetables that aren't nutritionally supplemented by insect proteins. But a wheelbarrow? No, these days I pile everything I need into an old bed sheet and drag it around the garden or to the burn pile. An old sheet is light and much easier to store and move then the single-wheeled torture devices created by a medieval sadist or the modern four-wheeled gardening carts that can retail for approximately as much as a new car. A leaf rake is now a thing of the past for me as well, replaced by the mulching lawn mower which simplifies greatly the chores of fall as well as providing valuable mulch for the lawn. Plant native adapted plants or xeriscape and you can forget all you ever learned about garden hoses and sprinklers and soaker hoses. I do recommend keeping a bucket around for holding stuff and carrying it around the garden (fertilizer, tools, water, etc.)

My Best Advice

I'm not a gardening expert, I just play one in my fantasies and in my occasional Master Gardener role in the community. So take the advice which follows as the voice of bitter experience, but not as a proclamation from God on High. These are certainly mainly examples of "do what I say, not what I do." Because I know what's good for you, even if I can't see that it's good for me.

My foremost advice to other gardeners is to be ready and able to kill plants. I don't mean for you to plant them and then neglect them until they're brittle bark-less twigs in the garden. I mean that my human failing is that I am unable to cull and kill plants that I simply can't stand or that aren't doing well for me. I kill plenty of plants by ineptitude or poor care or neglect, but never the plants that I should kill. And as a result there are far too many plants in my garden that don't provide either utility or beauty or decent backdrop. In my garden, there is no death penalty, there is just death by accident. And whether or not doing without a death penalty is good for a human society, it's very bad for a good garden.

There are very few plants that I've ever brought into my garden that I have later tried to eradicate and most of them are named in the chapter titled "*Gifts That Keep On Giving.*" If I don't like it, but it's not a completely vile plant, my usual response is to move it to somewhere where it is less likely to survive and where I don't have to look at it on a daily basis. This is akin to casting out irritating children into the cold to let them survive or perish on their own. Most human societies frown on the latter, and we should also frown on the same treatment to plants. For pity's sake, give it a swift painless death on the compost pile or exile it to someone else's garden rather than a slow drying out in the wind and sun. Occasionally moving the plant will place it in better surroundings and it flourishes there, but that is just painting over the sow's ear so the purse is blue instead of pink. A plant with poor flowers or poor form or poor foliage should just be eliminated. Cut the cord, give that dahlia away to the crazed dahlia fanatic down the street, or otherwise improve its contribution to the garden by making compost. Don't wait for all those purple-leaved trees to die, cut off a few, burn them as firewood, and replace them with normal trees. One of the only plants I've ever given away to get out of my garden was a brown-speckled Bearded Iris that I simply couldn't stand the sight of. I gave "a start" which happened to consist of my entire plant, to my Dad so that it was finally gone from my garden. And I've never regretted it. And I might not regret many of my other planting mistakes if I had but the courage to create a "final solution."

The only real exception to this death sentence should be when a plant needs moved because of color clash with its neighbors. I say that, but yet again, I rarely follow it in my own garden because by planting mostly pure colors instead of pastels, most of my garden flowers never clash with each other, they either contrast or complement each other. Most of the time, a plant that clashes in one area of my garden will clash in another, or even just plain looks ugly on its own. In truth, the Canadian rose 'David Thompson' is of a pink that I simply don't like but have tolerated for years. It sits between clear pink 'Carefree Beauty' and the old blush garden rose 'Fantin Latour' and although it really clashes with neither, it's just a color I don't like. It should be eliminated. Right now it's got several dead canes and seems to be partially dying. Perhaps it has sensed my dislike and is trying to eliminate itself. I have hope. Perhaps the hippies of the '60's were correct and plants can sense our moods and respond to them.

Regarding planting techniques, gardeners should be brutal to the roots of potted plants when transplanting or planting out. Cut them, tease them, spread them out, trim them, unwind them, and just plain squish them when planting into a new hole. I say "be brutal" because if I tell you to be brutal, most of you who normally wouldn't think of disturbing a root will at least do enough to get the roots to spread out. It's a bit on the same theory that as a veterinary orthopedic surgeon, I tell the owners of a dog I've fixed a broken leg on to restrict the exercise about three times longer than they really need to, figuring that I might then get them to restrict it just long enough. Tell them eight weeks, you get three weeks of exercise restriction when the dog really needs eight. Tell them sixteen weeks of exercise restriction when you really need eight weeks and you might get six weeks if you're lucky.

My third piece of best advice is to use indicator plants to tell you when a gardening chore needs to be done. For indoor plants, identify the first plant to wilt when unwatered and then water all your houseplants only when that particular plant is showing signs of stress, not on a weekly or twice-weekly or some other artificial schedule. Identify the rose that first gets blackspot and don't initiate spraying the other roses until you see blackspot on "the One." For me, that rose is the yellow rose "Captain Samuel Holland." When it sheds leaves, others are soon to follow. Likewise the first plant to get spider mites (for me that plant is a *Cotoneaster apicularis* or the native Rudbeckia). When that baby gets the little cobbery webs all over it, it's almost always late summer in the dry times and it's time to get the spider mite spray out.

Favorite Garden Writers

Many garden writers each have their own little eccentricities although some of them at times seem almost normal. I have formed images and impressions of all of them from their writing which may be accurate, but are more likely wholly a creation of my imagination. I can't really pick a favorite, but I'd like to outline a number of them that others may seek out and enjoy them as well.

I have recently discovered the esteemed Irish gardener and writer Helen Dillon, and I believe she will soon become one of my favorite writers. *Down to Earth* is her newest work, and I find the format of the book organized primarily into short two page essays to be very engaging to read. She touches on lots of different topics which jump from thought to thought, garden hint to garden observation. Helen has the enviable ability to slip in loads of useful information about plants and design seemingly without meaning to or without boring the reader as if one was reading from a botanical dictionary. I see Helen as the contemporary neighbor who is good and gardening and frequently wanders to the fence to provide some advice. Many of her thoughts are the echoes of my own (or vice versa) and so I identify deeply when she discusses how tools seem to want to sprint for freedom the minute they're left alone, or how the potting shed is untidy and cluttered despite frequent cleanings. Her dry humor shines as when she talks about growing horsetails (*Equisetum hyemale*) in a pot "in case it gets out and tries to colonize Dublin." And many future and former organic gardeners will relate to her description of an array of insecticide containers as "the killing shelf of the potting shed," and to her statement that "There's nothing more satisfying than the squelching sound of a cluster of greenfly being squeezed between finger and thumb. Certainly quick and definitely organic."

One of the most thought-provoking relatively recent gardening books is Michael Pollan's first book written about gardening, *Second Nature*. In it, I find Michael to be that liberal philosopher friend we all have, the one who votes democratic in every election no matter how high the income taxes or how many times William Jefferson Clinton asks what "is" means. In *Second Nature*, Michael wrote a wonderful collection of essays that strike deep at the basic human urge to garden, from an essay on what happens to a garden after the gardener leaves and nature reclaims its own (beware of Dudleyville!) to a delightful story of the collective philosophy of suburbanites and how his father rebelled against the neighbors and his father-in-law. You can't help but visualize the image of angry neighbor's "hitting the gas angrily as they passed" (his father's unkept lawn), exhibiting "pithy driving, the sort of move that is second nature to a Klansman." He wrote a memorable essay about old garden roses and what they represent and say about the gardener's choices. How genuine is the chagrin with which he admits that he finds the old garden rose 'Madame Hardy' more chaste, more aristocratic and more poised compared to modern roses. How delightful is his description of the sexuality evident in the blossom of 'Maiden's Blush'. In *Green Thoughts,* the chapter "Weeds Are Us" is an interesting comparison of the global spread of weeds with the spread of Western human society.

Michael Pollan has written several other books of interest to gardeners. Mr. Pollan's second book *The Botany of Desire* was also enjoyable, discussing the origins of four domesticated species, the apple, the tulip, marijuana and the potato, and how they were selected by man from their wild origins to become the plants we see today. That sense of history, that story of man changing nature to fit his will can appeal to every gardener at some level. Michael even wrote a very delightful story of creating a writing retreat in *A Place of One's Own,* bringing voice to the urge of every gardener and writer to find or create a place of sanctuary to enjoy what they love. Unfortunately, I've enjoyed less his two most recent books, *The Omnivore's Dilemma,* and *In Defense of Food: An Eater's Manifesto.* Both, while interesting, become a little dreary and a little preachy on the subjects of environmentalism and our carbon footprints, a little too "Al Gore" in tone for my tastes. Michael, please, for us, go back to discussing your garden and your thoughts on gardening before Dudleyville claims your writing and your loyal audience.

Lauren Springer Ogden is perhaps the current best of the revolutionary crew writing about gardening today. She is also, in my mind if not in person, a beautiful and intelligent modern woman with a work ethic that defies belief. My admiration for her writing is such that my wife thinks I have a "thing" for Lauren and she's probably correct in that assumption. Her first book, *The Undaunted Garden,* is destined to become a gardening classic, if it's not already. I may be somewhat biased since she writes about plants and techniques that fit my climate zone and because the main premise of the text is to promote plantings that survive the wind, hail, torrential rain, and droughts that alternate as climate for the Great Plains, but all in all, this is a ground-breaking book that points out the beauty of regional gardening knowledge. I have an original hardback copy of *The Undaunted Garden* that I refer to frequently for its excellent advice and I someday hope to meet Ms. Ogden and have it autographed. I also have copies of her second book *Passionate Gardening* written with Rob Proctor, and I'm about halfway through the recent *Plant-Driven Design* written with her husband and fellow horticulturist David Ogden. The former is a good listing of plant combinations and practices with essays written alternating between the two authors, but I'm less than enthused so far about the latter, which is a bit repetitious and preachy about putting the plants first in the design of our gardens. Don't get me wrong, I agree wholeheartedly with the premise, and the book is beautifully illustrated with pictures taken by the author of their gardens and gardens they have visited, but I just think the important information could have been clearly written in a couple of paragraphs in each chapter.

Sara Stein is another revolutionary garden writer who I envision as the older, stern school-marm intent on teaching us a better way. Sara's book pair titled respectively *Noah's Garden*, and *Planting Noah's Garden*, form a complete revolution on how we should garden related to native plantings and our relationship with native fauna. Ms. Stein's vision of the American lawn is quite different from modern suburbia in that she promotes wildlife habitat and corridors stretching across the United States from coast to sandy coast. It was a great influence in my former garden in the city limits of Manhattan, but now here on the prairie, protection from roving fires has demanded that I set my garden at least spatially separate from the prairie grass surrounding. Her ideas probably wouldn't be safe in Southern California either, but the deer and turkey populations would probably benefit elsewhere across the nation. Sara has another previous work I'd recommend to all gardeners that is entitled *My Weeds*. *My Weeds* deals with the philosophy regarding calling a weed a weed and also talks about the physiology and history of many common North American garden weeds. All in all, a very delightful and informative read on a cold winter's night.

Deep Mulching and Biodynamics

Among my many other failings as a gardener, I must confess a vague unease of any reading or practice that mentions or promotes "organic" gardening, and yet I strive at times to follow many of the practices of those who garden in an environmentally sound way. It's a strange dichotomy that I can't fully explain. On a conscious and open-minded level, I fully understand the benefits of maintaining the natural balance and processes of the soil, if only to take advantage of the millions of years of knowledge and ability that all plants have stored in order to fully utilize their environment. Manure tea, encouraging earthworm survival, mulch, and all the other tenets of organic gardening are well within my knowledge and means. But I am reticent to follow the lead of those enlightened and outspoken individuals who I often feel a just a bit on the nutty side. You may think "organic gardening" and see a vision of Eden with angels flying overhead. I think "organic gardening" and picture a wild-eyed old man or woman with unkept flowing gray main locks in khaki shorts and Birkenstocks shouting that we're dooming the planet.

This seems to be the day that the fates have conspired to force me to come to terms with what exactly it is that bothers me about what I know I should do. The local Sunday paper started it off with a column stolen from the Los Angeles Times entitled *Not Digging Any Deeper*, by a writer named Lisa Boone. It, of course, featured a gardener practicing a no-dig philosophy of deep mulching as advocated in Ruth Stout's *The Ruth Stout No-Work Garden Book*. The article also gave me a new vocabulary word, "locavore," undefined in the article, but defined by Wikipedia as "the practice of eating a diet consisting of food harvested from within an area most commonly bound by a one hundred mile radius." This term was just coined in 2005 by a group of San Franciscans, but I don't plan to follow the practice, both because I like peaches in winter even if they were raised in Brazil, and because I have no desire to follow anything conceived in San Francisco (unless we're talking about Natalie Wood or Barbara Eden). I've lately been turning more and more to deep mulch myself though, and I'll tell you, it's not without some measure of trepidation that I'm entering tree-hugger land. I first started mulching with straw in the vegetable garden and it appeals to both my lazy and cheap natures. I quickly found that I like the easier and less-frequent weeding that follows, and the need to water less, if at all, and also the neater appearance of the garden and the lack of topsoil erosion after heavy rains in my mildly sloped vegetable garden. And, as a side-benefit, straw in Kansas is easily obtained cheaply in large quantities year round and for the benefit of those who are city-borne, it comes conveniently packaged in this 2X2X4 foot rectangle called a "bale." Think of it as a less acidic and sustainable substitute for peat moss. The stuff grows earthworms like it was earthworm candy. And planting in the stuff is a snap. As Ruth Stout opined, one merely pushes aside the mulch and uses a Dutch hoe to make a nice planting furrow wherever one feels the need. I have a nice large-wheeled garden plough/cultivator that was once my grandfather's and despite my sentimental attachment to it and childhood memories associated, its now been hanging three years on my garage wall without use, beside the rototiller which also hasn't been used for a couple of years in my own garden (but which seems to be a favorite "borrowing" item by friends). Another good local substitute for straw is prairie hay, similarly cheap and also baled, but perhaps of less favorable appearance. I've liked it on my vegetable garden so much that I recently mulched a mixed perennial and shrub border with prairie hay, an experiment that should pay off quickly this summer in lower maintenance. Yea Gods, where's a tree, because I sound like I need a hug.

My day of enlightment continued with my Sunday dose of the HGTV show *Gardening by the Yard,* containing a segment on biodynamic agriculture with a young acolyte of Rudolf Steiner, prominently featured in his garden in his mandatory faded jeans and Birkenstocks. Now, previously, I'll admit that without real evidence I'd placed Steiner in the same mental file folder as I hold L. Ron Hubbard and his Scientology followers (not a "good" folder in case you're wondering). Before any gardener jumps in and begins swirling quartz crystals in water for an hour one direction and then another hour in the opposite direction in order to form a preparation for spraying on roses, one should perhaps read up on old Rudolf. An Austrian philosopher and follower of Goethe born in 1861, Rudolf Steiner founded biodynamic agriculture, anthroposophy, Waldorf education, anthroposophical medicine, and Eurhythmy. Wikipedia contains quite a lengthy description of Steiner's life and works. In reading it, I found myself desperately searching for evidence that Steiner was a complete nut, and yet I was unpleasantly surprised to find myself in agreement and admiration of a number of his life's work, causing a shift in that inner picture one maintains to a slightly more wild-eyed me. Waldorf education aims only at complete actualization of the individual and, as an educator, I can't fault the premise. Anthroposophy seems a bit out there, but again is a decent philosophy aimed at improving our spiritual connections with our physical world. Eurhythmy? Why fight a new form of dance and art with bias and disdain? I can't fault his motives and basic philosophy either; the Nazi's hated him and drove him out of Berlin, and I've always agreed with the premise that one of the best measures of character is who one has as enemies. Even biodynamics doesn't seem so far out at its base; sustainable agriculture as a basic premise and references to the "farm organism?" I can agree with those. And yes, growing plants according to the influence of heavenly bodies and applying dubious "preparations" to plants leaves us a little less solidly grounded in reality, but Steiner did, again according to Wikipedia, encourage his followers to scientifically verify his suggestions. As one trained in scientific method, I can't fault that either. Since the whole world seems to be moving towards Steiner, I think I'd better resolve to do a little more reading into the old boy.

Gifts That Keep On Giving.

Gardeners love to express their generosity by giving away extra plant starts, and many garden writers instruct us on how grateful we should be for these free gifts. Humbug. I'm here to tell you that the old adage about being aware of Greeks bearing gifts (i.e. Trojan Horses), should be changed in the modern age to "beware gardener's bearing gifts." And I'm not just referring to the truckloads of zucchini we gardeners drop off in the dead of night on unsuspecting neighbors and friends because this year we happened to plant two zucchini seedlings instead of the usual one. No, I'm talking about those garden acquaintances that provide us with a beautiful specimen from their own garden that we have no way of declining lest we appear ungracious. These individuals, hereafter known as the "Fiends", provide these plants seemingly as unknowing or uncaring as Typhoid Mary that they are the source of a plague of infestation. It is my current suspicion, however, that these gifts are provided while the beneficent gardener is suppressing a good belly laugh.

We should know better, you and I. As a general rule of thumb, any plant prolific enough to allow another gardener to pass on extras is, by definition, a rampant pest. If it lives and grows that well under the care of the average gardener, I guarantee it will be hard to eliminate by the time we realize it's strangling the roses and about to pull off the downspouts. Those plants which are treasured, truly rare and hard to grow are kept by elite gardeners as status trophies and never passed on or shared. My current advice is to run screaming from any plant offered freely unless you have seen how the plant grows in your area and in all conditions for at least five years. And if given a plant you can't refuse at the time for reasons of decorum, isolate the thing until it can be doused in a bucket of gasoline and then immolated.

I, for one, curse the day and the gardener that gave me the native wildflower *Commelina diffusa*, also known as the climbing dayflower or spreading dayflower. I was but a novice gardener, viewing the garden of a friend of my wife, when I spied the healthy succulent foliage and beautiful sky-blue blue tri-lobed flowers of *Commelina*. I swooned, as I was then, as now, a sucker for that sky-blue color. The Fiend who grew it didn't seem to know it by name (else the *diffusa* species name might have been a hint to both of us if we had known its scientific name), but immediately offered me a start and assured me that it would grow well in our area, surviving in dry shady areas. And it did. I took it home to my first garden, where in the shade, for a season, it behaved itself. I became quite attached to the little creature, and when we moved soon thereafter, I made sure and placed a start from the plant into the vegetable garden on our new land so that I could transplant it later as the garden developed.

It was there, in the sun, that I learned the true nature of the Spreading Dayflower. It can't be killed. Neither hoe nor mulch nor cold nor herbicide will stay this monster from its appointed conquest of the planet. The only difference between this stuff and kudzu is that glyphosate will kill kudzu. Before I transplanted it to the rest of my garden, it was two years in the sun where it seems to have responded to sunlight like the fictional Andromeda Strain, and luckily I had realized its true nature was to smother any other plant in its immediate vicinity. When I realized it was a problem, and after finding the normal methods (hoeing, pulling, herbicide, or atomic bomb) didn't eradicate it, I looked it up in search of finding its Achilles heel. I identified its true name and learned only that it has no weaknesses. The USDA plant database identified it as weedy and invasive. Government scientists are nothing if not understated.

It's now been nine years since I introduced *Commelina* into the vegetable garden. You've read the advice about keeping invasive plants chopped off at soil level to starve the roots? Doesn't work with *Commelina*. For seven years, every time I've seen the slightest seedling, the slightest sprig resembling a toddler of this plant, I've wiped it out. I've pulled it, sprayed it, hoed it, cursed it and urinated on it. Last night there were (I counted) seventeen new starts of this plant in the garden, ranging up to thirty feet from where the sole source was initially planted. It comes up through mulch six inches thick and likes to hide among the leaves of my strawberry and potato patches. I believe it's doing it all by underground runners because I don't believe it ever went to seed. In fact, due to how hard it is to eradicate and where it's popped up, I have nightmares that down deep in my garden soil there's a throbbing mass of *Commelina* plotting overthrow of the garden hierarchy, biding time until it can strike. If there is any consolation, it's that it doesn't seem to be able to go beyond the disturbed ground of the vegetable garden and survive in the neighboring prairie grass, and that it's about fifty yards to my first perennial bed. So, it's presently contained and I've got patience. It's either *Commelina* or me, and surely something will work. I recently found that *missouriplants.com* states that it "can be cooked and eaten". Unfortunately this site doesn't say if the gardener will curl up, vomit, and croak after the meal. Websites can be so unhelpful.

There's always the old adage, if you can't beat them, join them. A few days ago I found three 'Tiger Eyes' sumac seedlings near the parent plant and potted them up. I was contemplating just this morning who I was going to give them to as gifts. 'Tiger Eyes' is a currently popular, beautiful and useful garden plant with great summer chartreuse and fall orange foliage and many of my friends will love to have one. And I've got three plants I obtained from suckers for the mere price of potting them up. It fleetingly passed my mind that 'Tiger Eyes' is related to the smooth sumac endemic to our area that can spread underground to clumps covering complete acres and which I annually spray to keep out of my pastures. But I discarded that thought with a fiendish little smile and went back to choosing who I would bestow with the honor of a seedling to forever grace their garden.

Giving Gifts continued

There are, of course, other ways for unsuspecting gardeners to be lured into the fight of their lives with invasive plants. One such way is by reading the glowing accounts of a plant in a commercial nursery publication. I, who would not so much as dream of believing a single mercenary word in a car commercial or newspaper ad, am quite gullible when it comes to the flowery descriptions in colorful gardening catalogues. Why don't I see there is no difference between those trying to sell us carbon credits for global warming and those trying to sell the next got-to-have plant? Both, after all, are simply in it for the money.

I didn't suspect trouble though, from a group as highly esteemed in gardening circles as the Seedsaver's Exchange. Several years ago, I came across in my Seedsaver's catalogue a delightful entry on the Sunberry (*Solanum burbankii*), a small garden berry with the eminent background of being bred by none other than Luther Burbank in the early 1900's. As the story goes, good ole Luther had sold it to a dealer who introduced it to commerce as the Wonderberry. While critics believed Luther had merely reintroduced *Solanum nigrum*, the Garden

Huckleberry, Luther claimed his creation was a cross between *Solanum guinense* and *S. villosum*. Regardless, the catalogue text read "fruits are blue, slightly sweet and slightly larger than a pea. Said by its admirers to rival and even surpass Blueberries. The price was only $2.50 a packet, a mere pittance for such a historical treasure bred by the great Burbank.

Admit it, from that description, you want some too, don't you? As fruit-loving as my family is, and since my soil is too alkaline for blueberries, I couldn't resist growing something as good or better. I ordered a packet and planted it, even though I was slightly worried about eating anything related to the Nightshade family. But it grew well and soon the first berries ripened and after the dog seemed to consume them without harm and the children seemed to enjoy them, I also chanced to find them sweet and flavorful. I ate quite a few that first year, but I didn't consider it to be all that great and tired of picking the tiny fragile berries and I neglected on purpose to save seed for the following year.

On average, in my soil, I have troubles starting plants from seed until I learn their specific requirements and timing for planting, and I should have gotten a clue of the trouble to come from how easily the Sunberry grew the first time I planted it. The very next season, there was a familiar look to many of the weeds that popped up in the garden and sure enough, I realized that my visiting Sunberry had come to stay. I made sure to grub out every seedling as it became visible, and I keep it from going to seed religiously. What the catalogue had failed to mention was that the seed had the infinite survivability of lotus seed. Five years later, it's still popping up across the garden. I noticed yesterday that there were seedlings among the potatoes and onions near where it was originally planted, and also thirty feet away among the blackberries. And all for only $2.50 a pack.

Another way to obtain a death-defying plant is to succumb to its appearance at the local garden nursery. I'm always on the lookout for unusual plants, and a few years back I chanced across Symphoricarpos 'Spun Sugar', a variegated and cultivated form of the plant also known as snowberry or coralberry. There seems to be some confusion on the species name, since I've found it listed as both *S. orbicularis* and *S. orbiculatus*. Although it was labeled a spreading shrub, I thought that its variegated leaves and supposed red winter berries would make it a useful garden addition. It might have if it had performed as promised. It never produced a single berry that I observed in four years or even a flower. Its leaves dropped in winter and left a tangled ugly mass of fine brown twigs. Instead of the 3-4 feet noted in references, mine never got over about two feet tall, and within two years it had begun to spread over six feet in diameter and choke out neighboring plants. It would indeed, as one reference suggested "be best in a natural setting in the garden." Especially if one planned for that natural setting to eventually be a large ugly thicket of impenetrable coralberry. And so I ripped it out. And ripped it out. And found that it would spring up anew from any fragment of the roots left in place. Roundup, I think has finally claimed this one. Score one for the unsuspecting gardener.

Of course, not all acquisitions from the local nursery are as easily dispatched. To be fair, I was warned that *Houttuynia cordata 'variegata'* could be slightly invasive, but I saw it only as a great groundcover. There is a real tipoff if I've ever heard one; "a great groundcover." Those three words are gardener's code for "rampant invader reminiscent of Genghis Khan and his Huns." I had also heard that Houttuynia could have an objectionable odor if crushed. No problem, I wasn't planning to kneel down and smell it. Oh, the naiveté! What I got of course was a great groundcover that survives well in Kansas and when stepped on releases an odor of dying carcasses for upwards of ten square yards. Not a groundcover you want growing on the path between you and the hose faucet that you need to get to on a daily basis. It had to be eliminated and I'm still working on accomplishing that six years later. This plant is not only reluctant to expire, it also avenges each stem I pull up, leaving a scent on my hands that sets dogs to running from my presence and my wife to casting suspicious sniffs in my vicinity. I've reduced it to occasional leaves that sneak from underneath a protecting shrub but I remain ever vigilant for outbreaks in the same manner as the CDC watches for smallpox epidemics. Supposedly both have been eradicated, but one never knows for sure.

Yet a third way to gain a permanent visitor is to allow a volunteer native plant that you suspect may have redeemable qualities to flower in your garden. In that manner, I acquired the Showy Evening Primrose (*Oenothera speciosa*) in my strawberry patch this year. The Showy Evening Primrose is native to this area of Kansas, and it is indeed a splendid sight as it opens pure white in the evening and stays open through the morning, wisely closing in the heat of the Kansas day. It flowers on the prairie through May and June and those flowers provide the delicate refined qualities needed at times to offset the harshness of other prairie flowers. Unfortunately, while it behaves itself in native dry chalky soils, it becomes an invasive weed in cultivated soil. I have it growing well-behaved in my perennial beds where I encouraged its establishment, but this year I noticed a familiar foliage trying to establish a foothold in my strawberries. I was suspicious when I saw it rapidly spread across three rows, seemingly leaping the straw between rows as if by magic. When it bloomed, I instantly recognized the plant and the problem and began my usual pattern of pulling it when it was near desirable plants and spraying with herbicide when it had the audacity to appear in clumps on its own. I anticipate victory within two to three years, but I will have to remain ever vigilant against this one as well as immigrants constantly attempt to cross the border of my electric vegetable fence. A weed may indeed be defined as any plant that is growing where we don't want it, but in the case of the Evening Primrose, I view it as a weed that grows everywhere unless I intervene.

Big Mistakes

I believe it's helpful to readers of a garden book if the writer lists some of the bigger errors he's made in order to serve as an example of what not to do. In keeping with my own advice, I'd like to pop in a few ideas that didn't turn out nearly as well as they were intended.

The first and biggest mistake I've made to date in gardening (one never knows when a bigger one will come along and readers of this tome aren't likely interested in my mistakes outside of gardening) is the mistake of thinking that purple-leaved varieties of trees were unique and in vogue. This mistake is compounded by the numerous gardening catalogs which reach the mailbox weekly and which include only the rare and strange varieties, not accounting for taste. I have finally realized that purple is not better than green, it's just different. And too much of it can be a landscape nightmare. Don't get me wrong, I think a purple European Copper Beech (*Fagus sylvatica var. purpurea*) would be just the thing for a large landscape, having seen a mature specimen at Rose Hill Garden in the Bronx, but one can fall into a trap by admiring other purple-leaved trees. I looked for purple-leaved trees initially for my front yard thinking that the purple would complement the red brick of the house well. I woke up one morning this year to realize that most of the deciduous trees planted in my front yard were purple and the effect was depressing. Two varieties of purple-leafed crabapples and a *Prunus candedensis* 'Canada Red' dot the front yard and that's simply too much purple. Add in a 'Rosehill' white ash (*Fraxinus americana* 'Rosehill') in the front that turns maroon in autumn and it's entirely too much purple. One wonders what happened or what is wrong with plain green trees? Such is the cost of fanaticism and thoughtless impulses.

The 'Canada Red' tree in fact seems to have been so depressed this year by all the purple in my yard that it seems to have committed suicide to remove itself from blame. I can't remember where I got it, but it's an unusual tree for this area that I've liked for itself, bearing nice white flowers in the spring with a good scent, and growing rapidly to help establish the new landscape. The first tree I planted at the new house, it has grown steadily, if somewhat bulky, and it did provide the desired purple to complement the brick, even though I've been growing tired of the purple. This year, though, I thought it was becoming a bit weedy and pruned the tree to its three strong core branches in early spring. In the first wind storm, one of the main trunks came down, leaving the tree a bit lop-sided. I wrote that one off to happenstance. In the second wind storm two weeks later, another trunk came down, as if by pruning the outer wild growth I had exposed the inner growth to the full force of the wind. And sure enough, the third wind storm of June took out the remaining trunk. By that time, I rejoiced, both because I didn't need to make a decision to remove the tree (I have a weakness for not giving up even on hopeless and undesired plants), and because I could replace it with my current tree lust; a paper-bark birch. At least the purple is gone.

The two purple crabapples, 'Royalty' and 'Red Baron' remain, but I'm hoping a good storm takes out at least one of them. I chose both because I thought their pink and burgundy blossoms were better than the common white of most crabapple varieties at the time. The purple leaves of both, especially purple in the 'Royalty, were just a bonus. What I didn't foresee was that the burgundy blossoms don't really stand out from the spring leaves as I'd hoped, and so I can hardly tell now when the trees are blooming. Note to self; burgundy-pink blossoms will be more impressive against green leaves. Take a lesson from me. Too much new and different, and especially plants with dark foliage, is not a good thing. I suppose the same can be said for chartreuse-foliaged plants and variegated foliage. A few here and there in the landscape makes a nice accent to the greens of the garden. Too many of them and the garden begins to look like a freak show.

Another one of my great mistakes was to become too enamored by the low-maintenance carpet of buffalograss around my home. Seeing it do well, I resolved to try it out as a care-free groundcover for a rose bed and as groundcover for a bed with lilacs and forsythia. It did indeed do well for one or two years, but it necessitated mowing a large area periodically with a string trimmer as the lawnmower can't get into the areas. Since mowing with a string trimmer is not on my top ten list of favorite pastimes, I mowed it too low and too infrequently to benefit the buffalograss and thereby I encouraged weeds. And of course, as soon as the roses and lilacs grew large, they shaded the buffalograss and killed it, leaving behind several faster-growing and weedier prairie grasses which I now have to mow on the order of every other week less they smother the roses. Just this week I abandoned the experiment and began mulching the bed with grass clippings. Take it from me, buffalograss is not a groundcover for anything but a lawn.

While we're talking about great mistakes, I might as well fess up to a major landscaping fiasco having to do with hardscape. I believe I should start a support group for those who built a brick house and allowed the builder to put in grey concrete walkways. I have them and can't stand them. Why I didn't insist on a brick walkway to the front, I'll never know, but if you're making the choice because of your building budget, I can only suggest that you should resolve to walk through the mud until the proper complimenting walkway can be afforded. I look at the walk every day and know that someday, one day when money is no object, I'll either have to resurface the walk with brick pavers or rip it all out and replace it with brick.

A like error in landscaping was initially building the front landscaping retaining wall out of white limestone blocks (dry stack) because it was the least expensive material available. I did the wall right, laying a footing of gravel and leveling the courses, but I never liked the result of a white-knee high retaining wall in front of a red brick house. I put up with this one for about four years, but soon hauled the limestone down to edge the perennial beds and replaced the wall with colored landscaping blocks that look much better. Expensive things are always worth waiting for.

Another error in my design psyche was exposed when I wanted to place a stone surface on the mudhole that existed between the deck steps and the walkway down to the back of the house. Since I had some native limestone eroding down out down near the pond, I hauled a number of these flat stepping stones up from the bottom, placed them on a relatively level earth surface, and then spread concrete between the cracks and watered it in, as was recommended in several "do-it-yourself" gardening books. It looked great initially, but the result, five years later, is the knowledge that native Kansas limestone doesn't always stand up to weather extremes and foot traffic well and so I've got a large area of pulverized limestone and cracking cement that is going to have to be redone in short order. I'm currently trying to decide between brick pavers or stamped concrete in the area, but first, I'm laying down a nice bed of sand and killing off the pack rats that undermined the previous stone.

I did wise up a little when it came time to put in a back patio. I still couldn't afford brick and didn't really want to deal with the cracks between bricks anyway, but I did have the foresight to put in a dyed, stamped concrete patio that looks like fine red sandstone and at least matches the house. It in fact turned out so good that the contractor uses it as a sales promotion and has brought other people over several times to view the patio. I should start charging him royalties.

Flint Hills Winter Gardening: "The Ice Storm"

Winter in the Flint Hills is usually dry. That's an understatement. The only thing that keeps Kansas from being a desert environment is the months of April through June. Of the twenty-seven inches of annual rain, we get about eighty percent in April through June and then it shuts down. Tight. As it goes into July there are often six or even eight weeks without a sprinkle and one hundred-plus temps. And then in September and October we usually get enough rain to call ourselves only a semi-arid climate. Often, there might be an occasional sprinkle or light snow dusting between Halloween and Valentine's Day. In the twenty years I've lived in Kansas, I've seen winters where the only snow was on Halloween. I've seen winters where the only snow was a blizzard on March 10th with fifty mile per hour winds and eighteen inches accumulation. I've seen winters with two feet of snow that lasts a month. I've seen winters where the only precipitation is in the form of an ice storm on Thanksgiving. White Christmases are unusual here in the Flint Hills. In fact, I've seen several Christmases where the outside temperature still reaches into the sixties and I'm gardening in shirt sleeves. We've always had at least one or two freezes by that time, and plants are dormant, but we often have a warm December.

Last winter, however, was the topper of them all. The end of the year containing The Freeze, that late freeze we received in April that knocked both garden and gardener on their ears, was the winter of "The Ice Storm" in Kansas. I was out of the state when a freak winter storm came through and dumped a solid inch to almost two inches of ice on everything, and I came back the next day to an Arctic wasteland. Coming back the long way from Omaha, where it had barely snowed, through Topeka to Manhattan, I saw entire miles of telephone and electric lines on the ground and without a single pole standing. Miles and miles in the early morning where not a single light shined except the headlights of other idiots like me who were trying to get somewhere. It was eerie and medieval in its breadth. My wife was in panic mode as she hadn't had electricity for twenty-four hours and it was another full day before we saw heat, but there were others in worse shape. I felt sorry for the people in the area; there were people in Kansas who didn't get power or heat for two weeks after that storm. But I felt just as sorry for the shrubs and trees.

Where "The Freeze" seemed to hit perennials the hardest, "The Ice Storm" was devastating to the woody plants. From the Nebraska line southward, I saw trees standing with naked trunks, limbs down in a circle around the tree like it was shedding a hair coat.

As I arrived home, my garden was a crystal cathedral, which would have been glorious except that it was rapidly becoming a flat crystal platter. Everything that wasn't propped up by solid steel was sagging towards the ground. Shrub's splayed flat in circles on the ground. Shrub roses had most of their canes broken off even while their orange hips decorated the icicles like glow lights from within. And the trees. The plight of the trees brought new meaning to understanding the garden in terms of evolution. Eastern Red Cedars were split everywhere and toppled over where they weren't split. Cottonwood trees were not down, but were standing as naked spars with their limbs dropped around their feet. In one fell swoop I lost two crabapples, the limbs on several peaches, and a pecan from my yard. All over town, trees were down and little did we know that the full cleanup of debris would last into spring. If we were spared at all, it was that the Ice Storm, once over, was not accompanied by much in the way of wind. It took a full week to melt, an entire week where I prayed minute to minute that the wind wouldn't come up and send the glass cathedral crashing down.

It was instructive that other trees, the oaks and walnuts and sycamores that make up the mature forests in this area, were stronger, standing stiff and firm under the weight. The weedy Osage Orange trees (*Maclura pomifera*), those hedge apple trees that the Kansas settlers had depended on for fence posts and Native Americans had used for bow wood, they weathered the storm without incident, seemingly uncaring that the rest of the world was in crisis. And the grasses and prairie forbs were all, of course, untouched by the ice; their growth points happily hidden deep in the earth in winter slumber. To see those landscape elements that best survived both The Freeze and The Ice Storm is to see the native Kansas plants, adapted to their climate, scoffing at the poor immigrants who don't have the fortitude or foresight to know that someday, The Ice would come again.

On Colors

Any addict knows that the first step to recovery occurs through admitting your problem. Okay, I will. I am a color snob. It is a term with such vile connotations that I've been reluctant to admit to it. I've resisted facing that reality for years, but there's really no denying it. Actually that's not being truthful either. According to my Webster's, "snob" is the description for a person who "pretends to have intellectual superiority." I think the key word here is "pretends." I don't pretend to think I'm superior at all to the poor bourgeois crowd who think magenta is God's gift to color coordination, because it's obvious I simply am clearly endowed with higher garden color sensibilities than the masses. I would further like to truthfully begin my twelve-step program to color coordination snobbery by admitting fully and loudly that I'm a color purist. I need my garden colors on the bright side. No tints please, for this gardener, no umbers, no shades. I prefer my reds dressed in cardinal, my yellows buttery sunshine, my blues all shades of the daylight sky in daylight. My whites need to be bleached, my oranges the rind of the ripened fruit. Violet must be cloaked royal, and green the color of the spring Irish hillsides. Foliage and flowers should match and blend, not vibrate and jar. Not for me the mauves. Not for me, pastels. Magentas make me want to flee to Yenta, fuchsias make me feel like puke-shia, and cyans make me long for die-in'. Taupe makes me feel dirty in the likely way that a closet pornographer feels (I mean by that, of course, the way a pornographer who hides his true trade likely feels, not the way a person feels taking surreptitious pictures of unpainted closets). The search through memory for the mere term and spelling of chartreuse can set my nerves on edge.

I believe my color senses are tainted by latent childhood traumas and frequent spousal collisions, the latter of which thankfully involve interior home decoration and not garden decorating. My earliest experiences with color combinations were from observing my mother's redecoration of our house after she took an extensive correspondence course on interior decorating. As that attempt at continuing education happened to be in the mid-1970's, the whole house became tints and shades of harvest gold and avocado green, two colors that I still believe are tolerable together only after the observer has imbibed extreme amounts of alcohol (and I don't drink). Today, despite our long and happy married life together, my wife and I regularly and fervently disagree about color, which I prefer to blame on her firm belief that taupe is the solution to everything and her inability (sweet as it is) to choose when faced with hundreds of pattern and color choices. Conversely, being trained as a veterinary surgeon has resulted in a mindset where making instant decisions is never an issue for me and so over the years we've reached a workable solution in decorating our home where I narrow the multitude of choices down to a few and then my spouse chooses between light-blue and medium blue to match the lavender chair. My teenage daughter has lately begun to add in her two cents about color choices in the home and generally, I find her recommendations are excellent, although saying so in public has not helped stem the budding mother-teen daughter wars to come. We all agree that color in the garden is my province and mine alone, a concession that works perfectly well at keeping harmony within the home and hearth.

The deepest cause of my compelling desire to match plant colors is more confidently ascertained than my vague unease over Harvest Gold, and I don't need a Freudian therapy couch to find it. I have an engraved and painful memory related to a nubile female classmate with whom I once participated in a state high school honor choir rehearsal and concert. This strawberry blond nymph had not previously appeared upon my pubescent radar screen but upon her appearance at the concert in what I vividly remember as an exquisite form-fitting cream dress with imprinted light strawberries, she immediately attained celebrity goddess status in my psyche to an extent possible only in the mind of a teenage male. Unfortunately, I had prepared for the evening concert by bringing a medium brown suit, chosen for me by my mother of course, and forgetting to bring socks, a hardship made unintentially worse by my parents who attended the evening concert and in an effort to be helpful brought along a pair of bright lime-green socks for me to wear. That alone might have not been a total calamity, but since I was in those years of growth where pants legs on boys are perpetually too short, the socks stood out like a neon sign throughout the remainder of the evening and the flames of budding romance on my mind died as quickly as if snuffed by a Kansas tornado. I probably should have undergone years of intensive therapy for the psychological trauma, but I have compensated adequately by making sure my garden color combinations are as impeccable as humanly possible, and indulging an occasional craving for fresh strawberries. In fact, I would never even recall the incident except the daily necessity to choose whether to wear a white or robin egg blue shirt with my black pants, black socks, and black shoes.

No gardener, of course, can match all the flowers in a garden perfectly, but I recommend, nay I demand, that the blue-reds stay on one side of the garden and the yellow-reds the other. Keep your pinks away from my chartreuse, please. And don't let me catch you mixing burgundy and orange together. With all due respect to Elisabeth Sheldon and Dency Kane's opinions in *The Flamboyant Garden*, glaring, edgy combinations belong only rarely in a garden. Now let's all go out there and separate our whites from our colors, shall we?

Compost

Yes, I have a compost pile. In fact it's a glorious picture-perfect large compost pile made using castoff but functional pallets and filled up with bags and bags of perfect forest leaves. I know all about the 2:1 ratio of brown to green (I use weeds from the garden and lawn clippings as the green), about inoculating the pile with soil or old compost, about keeping the pile moist (about as moist as a wrung out dishrag), about turning or aerating the pile, and even about taking the temperature of the pile (which I don't do because that would be work and might make me the subject of spousal ridicule). However, I have yet to take a shovelful of compost from the pile. Now that may be because it's a new pile and hasn't yet reached the matured phase. And it may be that I don't want to dig all the way down the pile to see if the bottom is ripe. But it's primarily because I want the appearance of being an organic gardener without the hassle. Do you know how many people have commented and complimented me on my compost pile? How impressed visitors are with its size? How I don't tell them that I haven't yet got compost from it (and don't really want to shovel and wheelbarrow the stuff around my garden)?

Prior to this year, I confess that I didn't compost. "Gasp," you say? Yes, I threw kitchen scraps into the garbage disposal, newspapers into the trash bin, and, thankfully, I didn't have enough leaves off my young trees yet to fill a bucket. And as noted elsewhere (see the essay titled *The Truth about Low-Maintenance Gardens*), I have a basic lazy streak and don't want to do anything approaching work for work's sake. Make a pile of trash, which must be chopped up into tiny pieces, kept moist, and turned frequently? All to gain a few shovelfuls of rotten material to act as fertilizer with a nitrogen level about 1/8th of that in the $10.00 bag of lawn fertilizer? Get real. I resolved that if I wanted compost, I'd buy it at the nursery.

Well, the truth is that the bagged compost at the nursery, usually labeled as composted cow manure, is primarily a bag of wet smelly clay with little means within to improve the tilth of the soil it is applied to. And cotton-burr compost available some places looks and feels nice, but it's a trifle on the expensive side. There is also municipal compost in my area, available free at our county transfer station (otherwise known as the town dump). Theoretically, the county collects all those bags of leaf waste in the fall and composts them in long wind rows until the perfect decomposition has taken place. I admit that I once loaded up a pickup truck load of this stuff, brought it home and added it to a bed that currently contains a dozen 'Green Mountain' boxwood (*Buxus sempervirens X Buxus microphylla var. koreana*). That bed grows well today, making a nice shrub line to outline the drive in front of the house. But I won't do it again. As that municipal compost aged, rocks and other foreign objects became visible that left me happy I hadn't added it to the vegetable garden whose produce I eventually plan to eat.

So I've started my own compost pile essentially because I can't trust my fellow gardeners and nursery people to provide me good, really organic compost. I'll try it out for a while, see how it goes and how much work it is. The scientist in me will put compost on half my roses in my formal rose bed and just mulch the other half with straw to see if it makes any difference. The environmentalist in me will feel happy that I'm doing something for the Earth. It's for the children. The conservative Republican in me will make fun of the wacko environmentalist. And I'm not going to buy a rotating plastic compost bin. Or the Swedish-designed ramped composter I saw advertised earlier. Or a stainless steel compost fork. Or a compost thermometer.

If I have a real composting philosophy that I follow, it's the "compost-in-place" school of Ruth Stout. I've become over the years a devotee of Ms. Stout and my vegetable garden is mulched with piles of straw. Pulling back the straw and planting in the rich moist earth exposed each spring is perfect for me. No or little weeding and watering in the summer heat is also for me. As mentioned elsewhere, I also follow the premise that if I pull a weed, I throw it down to decay in the same place it grew, figuring that the best way to return those nutrients to the soil is to leave them there. Despite the fact that it rankles my wife to occasionally find a dead, intact weed lying around (or maybe because of it), I persist in this ultimate weeding laziness.

Currently, all my perennial beds save one are mulched with cypress bark mulch. Setting aside the environmental consequences of using bagged and unsustainable cypress mulch, I really just hate paying for and transporting several hundred bags of mulch yearly to my grounds. I've also noticed that I've built up about six inches in some places of this mulch and it's not breaking down very fast, forming a water penetrable but cake-like crust that must be chipped off for new plants. This year by happenstance, I obtained some old prairie hay from a friend and designated it for a perennial bed previously covered by about one inch of purchased cypress mulch and I've so far adored the results; I've not watered the bed at all and I bet I haven't pulled three weeds all summer in a bed that is approximately eight feet by sixty feet. Yes, the color of the rotted prairie hay isn't the nice reddish-brown of new cypress mulch, but neither is cypress mulch very pleasant to look at once the Kansas sun has bleached it over a couple of months.

I've liked the hay so much in fact, that I bought a bagger for my lawnmower and have begun using the lawn clippings to mulch beds previously unmulched. Since most of my lawn is mown prairie grass, it's really just prairie hay with less seeds. So far, a couple of mowings have mulched my formal rose bed and a large informal shrub rose hedge. And I've discovered that all the garden writers who have written not to use grass clippings for mulch are full of crap. It doesn't shed water, it smothers the heck out of weeds, and earthworms love it. What could be better?

More Garden Writers

No discussion of great modern garden writers would be complete without including the vivacious and bawdy and perhaps menopausal Cassandra Danz. Ms. Danz, the author of *Mrs. Greenthumbs* and *Mrs. Greenthumbs Plows Ahead* is a flirtatious writer who peppers some very good garden advice with bawdy comments about sweaty muscular garden apprentices, settling always for second best though on her seemingly meek husband, Walter. It's a new literary genre, this combination of soft porn and gardening, but one must read carefully or many of the cleverest references to garden bliss sail right over their hat. Ms. Danz, also a known comedienne, seems to overheat easily in the garden and, one would guess, just as easily in with indoor plants, but she always pulls it together to get her point across. Some of the best practical gardening advice I've read comes from Cassandra, highlighted by her chapter in *Mrs. Greenthumbs* on the colors of daylilies at a distance ranging from orange, to orange, despite catalogue descriptions to the contrary.

I enjoy few other garden writers as much as Sydney Eddison and Mirabel Osler, two grand dames of gardening who I have placed in my mind as the caring great-aunts who dispense loads of hard-fought wisdom as they putter in their gardens. Mirabel has a couple of classic garden philosophy entries in *A Breath from Elsewhere* and *A Gentle Plea for Chaos*. Sydney is a more wide-ranging author but I've never found a text of hers that isn't exquisitely readable. She gives a clear discussion on color in *The Gardener's Palate*, perfect entry-level discussion in *The Self-Taught Gardener* and a classic discussion of winter gardening in *The UnSung Season*. Given all that, though, Ms. Eddison hits her stride when talking about her first love, daylilies, in a number of gardening articles in magazines and in her landmark *A Passion for Daylilies*. I defy any gardener to read the latter without immediately afterwards running out to purchase a few new daylilies to stick into a corner. Ms. Eddison inspired me to explore spider daylilies, doubles, and miniatures to the benefit of my garden, and she also makes exquisite sense of the mysteries of diploid and tetraploid nomenclature.

Although male members seem to be missing from the ranks of the best garden writers (pun intended), there are a couple of excellent writers of garden essays that no reader can do without. My favorite essayist of all time is the late Henry Mitchell, former garden columnist of the Washington Post. Several collections of Henry's best columns have been compiled, including *The Essential Earthman*, *One Man's Garden*, and posthumous *On Gardening*. There is no one better to expose a garden's failings or to depict human foibles superimposed on garden designed than Mr. Mitchell. Writing always in a dry wit, with a curmudgeon's view of humanity, Henry draws us into agreement on favorite plants, inadequate landscapes, and pets, especially dogs, in the garden. The garden world would have been poorer without Henry Mitchell. Allen Lacy, on the other hand, is a philosophy professor who has authored at least ten books on gardening, among which are such classics as *Homeground*, *In a Green Shade*, and *The Garden in Autumn*. Firmly acquainted with plants, Dr. Lacy is also just as well acquainted with movers and shakers from all garden paths. Many of his essays describe the work of plant fanatics around the world, from those adventurers who collect plants in out-of-way corners of the globe, to those who grow *Monarda* in large quantities for commercial sale. He dabbles in design and garden display in *The Garden in Autumn* and thus expands home gardeners, much like Sydney Eddison's *The Unsung Season,* into other colder seasons separate from spring and summer of garden lushness.

Daylilies: not just another pretty flower.

Gardeners tend to be a choosy lot. A rose fanatic here, a hosta aficionado there, a landscaper dedicated to xeriscape gardening way over there, and we can find ourselves limiting the beauty available from our partnership with nature. While my own tastes are fairly eclectic as to plant species (except, of course, for my uncompromising dislike of the lowly spireas), I have been fairly selective for color and form and growth habits within a genus, and nowhere have I tended to be more selective than in the choice of daylilies to include in the garden. My innate disdain for the brassy oranges of daylilies has lead me to select for the most part only the best and clearest purples, reds, pinks and whites as the daylily winners in my gardening lottery. I also confess a lust for the ringed and eyed forms epitomized by many of the Shalom series and a number of them are distributed throughout the landscape.

Luckily for my garden, however, balanced against my color bigotry is my innate preference for landscaping on the cheap, so even while selecting for the best colors, I have also accumulated a number of the brassy oranges and yellows. In fact, the fantasies of daylily breeders and growers lend themselves to making such mistakes as pointed out best by Cassandra Danz (the famed Mrs. Greenthumbs). Mrs. Greenthumbs translates daylily color terminology quite accurately into reality, pointing out that accolades such as "melon"="orange", "peach" = "light orange", and "deep red"= "looks like orange from a few feet away." So when browsing the annual local daylily sale, which fills dual roles as a wonderful fundraiser for the local Daylily society and as a socialistic institution providing cheap daylilies to the masses, one inevitably chooses a number of "melon" daylilies that are quite frankly orange from more than six inches away. There are loads of the latter in my garden as in many others, but if one is choosy and not to attached to living things for life's sake, then one can select for as near favorite colors as allowed on the daylily scale. It's even worse if one tries to choose daylilies from a nursery catalogue or specialty grower, as mere mortals don't understand the cataloguese these are written in and thus, again, mistake "melon" for a color that won't look orange from three feet away.

Stop! Put away that spade! Put down the Roundup! Beauty is, doubtless, in the eye of the beholder, but just as the random gawky freckled teenager can be recognized later as a beautiful model, even the lowly Kwansi can have its moment. As a general rule of thumb, I now propose that gardeners should refrain from choosing daylilies based on any current preference for color or form, but we should accept all available and affordable *Hemerocallis sp.* and allow them to earn a place in our gardens by their performance over a period of years lest we miss the joys of unappreciated beauty. This is not because I believe that, one hundred years after the fall of civilization the remaining plants in Kansas will be buffalo grass, peonies and daylilies. It's because sometimes, just sometimes, our preferences for garden plants can change on a whim. Mrs. Greenthumbs describes ordering one hundred bargain daylilies which led to a daylily bed of "orange everywhere", but among these she found six daylilies that were not bright orange which ultimately cost $5 apiece after culling the 94 daylilies that were. Big deal, we commonly pay that much and for new cultivars we've not ever seen, so what is it really worth for a plant we've seen and know we like? Sometimes, we may find that in this year, this particular year because of some varity of weather or drought, a little-noticed variety will shine. This year, my evolution as a gardener took a turn and I found myself enjoying a number of daylily colors and forms that I previously thought beneath my garden décor. Tastes change, and although I still have disdain for the orange of Stella de Oro and prefer what I term "clear" colors, I found myself admiring a few of the melons, and many of the lighter yellow daylilies as a welcome change to the lack of bloom brought on in a late freeze. These cheery visitors have brightened many a spot this year in the garden and some of the more subtle tones and ringed forms have shined in their own spot. I'm very glad now that many didn't succumb to the spade in the past season.

I take heart that I'm not alone in my bias problems. The aforementioned local Daylily society puts up an annual display in the mall that is calculated to entice innocents and noviates into the web of daylily madness during the weakened state of most gardeners in mid-summer. I noticed in a recent newspaper article about the annual display that a quoted local grower noted proudly that the daylilies displayed were only the "best" hybrids and that the common "ditch lilies" were not represented. Those readers belonging to oppressed minorities will immediately recognize the fascist sentiment as akin to the Czar's disdain for the local proletariat or Hitler's rationalization for eliminating the Jews. Common ditch lilies indeed.

Self-Seeders

Self seeding plants are undoubtedly Eden's last remaining gift to gardeners. By self-seeding, they demonstrate their ability to thrive in our particular combination of temperature and moisture extremes, to be resistant to the natural insect predators of the region, and, above all, they are free to the cash-strapped gardener. Self-seeders may be invited guests, or they may be native invaders, but they relieve the gardener of the choice of where they will grow best by simply growing and leaving the gardener to remove them where they're unwanted.

In fact, controllable self-seeding plants add to the garden in a number of ways. First, they aid the organic or natural gardener by providing plants that look good despite minimal care or pesticide use in our climates. Second, in our quest to tie our gardens together by repeating plants or plant combinations throughout the garden, what better way to promote oneness in our garden design than by allowing self-seeding plants to repeat themselves and choose their favorite environs in our garden? And one cannot dismiss the fact that along with the native self-seeders come not only their flowers, but the native fauna that have evolved to utilize them and spread their seeds such as the butterflies and birds that depend on them.

I won't enter long into the controversy or definition of what constitutes a weed in a particular garden, except to say that I don't consider most self-seeding perennials as weeds. Weeds have been defined in various gardening texts using language that either depicts them as despicable thug-like members of a certain group of plants to simply being any plant that is not in a desired place. In practice, I only view as weeds those plants who are not only unwelcome, but who insist on staying at the party despite all efforts to thrust them out the door. Self-seeders, by contrast, may crash the party, but they usually end up adding to the party atmosphere by their vivaciousness and we can often get them to leave the party when they get drunk and unruly merely by showing them the door.

In my own garden, I welcome a number of native perennial forbs whenever and wherever they show up. Growing in the prairies around me are desirable natives *Asclepias tuberose* and *Salvia azurea*. The bright orange butterfly weed (*Asclepias tuberose*) grows from one to three feet tall in this area and has a long flowering period from June through August. As the name suggests, it draws all sorts of native butterflies during the flowering period like teenage males to a cheerleader practice. As desirable as the flowers of butterfly weed is the velvety light green erect foliage that provides a foliar contrast to more glossy or darker green perennials. Providing a delicious counterpoint to the bright orange butterfly weed is the blue sage (Salvia azurea), a three to five foot tall erect plant of light sky-blue in color that survives in dry native conditions and poor soil. Both these plants are difficult to transplant due to long deep taproots and thus they are easy to eradicate in unwanted areas by the gardener. Both grow for me in a number of places within the garden and I have learned to recognize and encourage the seedlings of both plants so as to increase their number throughout the garden. They grow as sub-perennials between roses and viburnums, or among the peonies to provide late-season counterpoint to the early-blooming peony bed.

Another perennial that I allow to self-seed throughout my garden beds wherever it pleases is a form of blue and purple columbines that grow particularly well at the shaded roots of large shrubs. In fact, I encourage these to spread by waiting until the seeds are ripe and then spreading them from bed to bed simply by shaking the seed pods around at the proper time. I also go through each year and grub out plants that bloom white or light lavender, leaving only the brightest blues and darkest purples to breed and propagate across the garden.

I also appreciate several self-seeding annuals that persist in my garden. A white flowering tobacco (*Nicotiana alata*) is a plant that I introduced once into the vegetable garden, and it since pops up occasionally in my perennial beds to provide nice nighttime focus with its glowing white flowers in the moonlight and the delicious sweet scent that spreads from it on the wind. I have also thought about allowing self-seeding of a double form of pink opium poppy (*Papaver somniferum*) given to my father years ago by a friend. The poppy is quite distinguishable from the native thistles by its thicker grey-green foliage and so it's easy to leave it growing wherever it pops up, often in dry inhospitable soil where other plants fear to grow anyway. Unfortunately of course, for those members of the DEA reading this narrative, I don't have seed for that particular poppy anymore.

Of Native Lawns

There is a fad in modern gardening circles to move away from high maintenance, over-fertilized, over-insecticided, over-watered bluegrass and fescue lawns in favor of native turf grasses, and for once I'm right in the forefront of fashion. I can quote all the bad press about how suburban lawns require more fertilizer, water and insecticide than grain farming in the United States and how poor a choice it is to grow Kentucky Bluegrass in most areas of the country and how much time we waste fertilizing and continually mowing our picture-perfect green lawns. I know people who have irrigation systems and who mow acres of lawn twice a week and I think they're nuts. But before you get a picture of me as a wild-eyed Al Gore devotee, you should know that my primary reason for choosing a native lawn is laziness. I don't like to traipse around behind a fertilizing cart, I don't like to drag hoses all over the lawn to water, I'm too frugal to install irrigation and pay for water, and I especially don't like to mow. Let me emphasize that if there's one thing I'd put at the top of the fruitless list, it's mowing the lawn. Forget environmentalism, native lawns save labor, or so the story goes.

When we built our current home on the prairie, I chose to start a buffalograss (*Buchloe dactyloides*) lawn around the house based on all the hype regarding the low-maintenance requirements of such turf. Stock Seed Farms of Murdock Nebraska (www.stockseed.com) is a retail establishment that specializes in native prairie grasses and forbs, and their advertisements can't be ignored. Straight from their website, they proclaim "Did you know Buffalograss requires almost zero maintenance? Buffalograss conserves water, and requires almost no watering or mowing. It makes a great lawn for the dryer areas of the Great Plains!" Man, that sounds like it's written for me. Unfortunately, my cynical scientific training flew out the window and I neglected to observe that you don't have to mow or water bluegrass either, as long as you don't care how it looks.

I didn't choose just any buffalograss. After carefully researching buffalograss lawns, I found that most of the available varieties at the time were established from plugs. Since I have neither the funds or patience to plant a few thousand plugs into my lawn, I searched high and low for buffalograss seed and came across the varieties 'Tatanka' and 'Cody' offered by Stock Seed Farms. Both were been bred by the Native Turf Group in cooperation with the University of Nebraska, and I suspect that a better pedigree couldn't exist. My neighbor, also into the low-maintenance stuff, chose to install a 'Cody' lawn and I chose 'Tatanka' knowing that it was a parent to Cody, but figuring mostly that a buffalograss named for buffalo was cool. And 'Tatanka' was more expensive than 'Cody', proof that it was better, right?

Buffalograss, as a warm-season grass, needs hotter germination temperatures than cool-season grasses such as turf-type fescues. We planted in the hot weather, kept the soil moist, and sure enough, we both soon had a decent stand of buffalograss. In the next few years, it filled out and became denser as promised. No fertilizing, no watering, and mowing at only two week intervals! And mowing only then because my wife didn't like the seed heads which popped up all over the lawn (low-maintenance seems to not be a part of the vocabulary of most wives). I was so enamored by the stuff, I decided to try buffalograss as the undercarpet to a couple of shrub beds, hoping to eliminate mulching under the shrubs (see the chapter titled *Big Mistakes*). And for several years, we both indeed had low-maintenance lawns, a bit browner in the winter and slower to green up in the spring, but allowing us the superior feeling obtained from telling friends we only mowed six times a summer. In my case, since the "outer" lawn was simply mowed mixed prairie grasses, forbs, and rocks, the buffalograss provided a nice contrast and transition by surrounding and setting off the house. And my children loved the fine texture of the stuff under their bare feet.

And then, in the third or fourth summer, trouble in paradise was evident. In the first place, it became clear in a couple of seasons that in fact, you don't HAVE to water buffalograss in the summer, but if you don't water you can expect that it will become brown and dormant in August in Kansas. It does green back up towards September as we get more rains and cooler temperatures, but the green-up is fleeting as it enters winter dormancy. Also in the third season, I first noticed areas of buffalograss were thinning out, and a prominent five foot circle at the beginning of the entrance walk became brown and denuded entirely. I suspected grubs but wasn't able to observe any. It also didn't seem to be the fungus (Brown-patch) I was accustomed to in K-31 yards. I raked the soil, fertilized, and watered in the bare area. Weeds came up, but little or no buffalograss made an appearance. I moved plugs from other parts of the yard to the area and they survived, but did little growing. My neighbor had similar problems and after a diagnosis of cinch bug infestation and weed overgrowth, began using both herbicide and insecticide on his grass. I persevered and began watering and fertilizing and soon the spots filled back in.

By the fifth summer I had realized the truth. Buffalograss is low-maintenance compared to many turf-grasses, but it is certainly not "no-maintenance." It benefits from both fertilizer (albeit at a lower application rate than cool-season grasses), and from yearly select herbicide use to eliminate broad-leaf weed competition. And in my area, occasional glycosphate should be spot-applied to kill cool-season invaders while the buffalograss is dormant in the spring. Cinch bugs remain a problem with some varieties (it seems worse with 'Cody' than 'Tatanka') and so insecticides cannot be fully eliminated. It isn't as dark green as turf-type fescues, but it does have a nice light blue-green look once you get used to it. And you don't have to water, but you'll have a nicer, thicker lawn if you support it with extra water in the heat of summer. And while you don't have to mow it and the seed heads are nice to look at, it doesn't really stay to six inches high in this climate, particularly if watered and fertilized at regular intervals. But that doesn't matter because while you can take the cool season out of the lawn, you can't take the cool-season lawn out of the wife and I therefore have to mow frequently enough to keep the seed heads down.

'Tatanka' has since been discontinued for reasons that I'm not aware of (and suspect may be due to those bare patches I experienced), but Stock Seed still offers 'Cody', and also 'Bison', 'Texota', and 'Bowie'. 'Legacy' is another variety high-touted, but it is seedless and available only in plugs. I know I may not have made the best case for it, but I'd choose Buffalograss again if I had the choice here on the prairie. One big advantage is that even though you'll see the occasional bare patch, it fills in rapidly if you pay attention. I fertilize twice a year, once in May as the stuff greens up and again in July just before the summer heat sets in. I use Dimension weed and crab-grass preventer in the spring on the turf and I spray broad-leaf herbicide in mid-summer to keep the weed competition down. I mow every other week, but I mow high and it forms an incredibly dense and fine-leafed turf. And most of all, merely stating that I have a buffalograss lawn makes the wild-eyed environmentalists swoon.

Dueling with Deer

It seems especially common in their writings for East Coast gardeners to lament their encounters with deer in their gardens. Less you think that Kansas is devoid of these large furry rats, I have had over the years a deer visitor (certainly not a <u>dear</u> visitor) who is uncanny for ticking me off and who I'm planning to donate as venison to a local kitchen as soon as possible. Or perhaps it's several sequential deer visitors over the years; an entire family of deer predisposed to aggravate me down through their generations. Regardless, I am also not without my own trials with even-toed ungulates of the family Artiodactyla.

In the pre-house days on the land we now occupy, one of my first goals was to begin to establish an orchard in the hopes of a long-off period of fruitful harvest. At that time, it was little more than fenced prairie with nary a neighbor in sight. One fine early spring day I mowed the grass and planted six fruit trees (a cherry, two peaches, and three apples) one evening, in a sloped area with good drainage and southwest exposure, one that I hoped would lead to frost-free fruit buds during the chilly spring Kansas mornings. I was careful to place the root ball at the proper depth in the midst of massive stone-moving efforts to clear out the prescribed planting hole to two times the diameter of the root ball as suggested by all authorities. The summer went on, the trees leafed and grew, and I kept mowing.

And then one day I returned to find two of the three apple trees devoid of leaves, just stems clinging to the branches. Strange, I thought. It seemed a particularly rapid denuding of the tree even though I had noted some cedar apple rust on one of the two. Two days later the third apple tree was naked in the yard. As winter was coming on, I felt nonplussed about the matter and resolved to spray for rust the next spring. Then I returned another day in November to find that the peaches and cherry tree trunks looked like they had been scraped bare with a paint scraper.

Deer damage trees in two ways; they damage the bark on the trunk of young trees as they sharpen their antlers during rutting, and they eat the new tender leaves and twigs in the spring. My deer are unusually talented and do both. In that first winter, the deer killed all but one tree, the latter of which barely survived a scarred up trunk to the velvet-tipped antlers of the rutting bucks and loss of most of its leaves to the velvet lips of the does. I was left with a number of small sticks placed in a regular pattern on the hillside and one sapling with three intact leaves. As a flanking maneuver, the deer also nibbled some newly planted thornless blackberry plants down to bare sticks. You know, it's one thing if the ruminant rodents would just chew things down to the ground, but no, they eat all the leaves and leave the decrepit stalks and trunks up to slowly starve to death.

I replanted and I learned that much of the advice you read in gardening books about repelling deer is crap. Hanging deodorant soap from the trees did nothing to deter the little cretins, nor did hanging sacks of human hair, nor did stringing video tape between poles around the trees (it's supposed to make a hypersonic noise that repels them, but mostly it just blows down in the Kansas wind), nor did spraying the trees with pepper spray. Trying to garden only with plants that deer don't consider tasty isn't an option, plus I've had them eat a 'Tiger Eyes' Sumac down to a stub, but haven't had it bothered since that one time, so I'm starting to believe that they just sample things at random and there is no real pattern of likes or dislikes in their palate. I do believe human urine in the immediate plant area is effective as a deterrent and it seems to work best if voided while one thinks angry thoughts about the deer or imagines the feel of venison juices running down our chin. But one gets tired of running outside to the orchard several times daily, particularly first thing in the morning while the dew is on the grass, and the neighbors start to give you sideways glances and talk in low whispers. Aside from urine, what really deters the doey-eyed night visitors is a high, solid or woven fence. Unfortunately, it leaves the garden and orchard looking like the demilitarized zones at the border of warring states (which it is).

The next year I replanted, surrounding all trees by a circle of woven-wire fence and fencing off the blackberry plants and found success. Only in the occasional twig which had ventured outside the cages did I see any signs of ruminant nibbling. The trees thrived, survived the subsequent Kansas summer heat and the ubiquitous cedar apple rust of this area, and made it through a long winter unscathed. It was in their second spring that I learned of the dangers of prairie fires as regards small trees. An escaped prairie fire from the neighbor's spring burn caught them just as they were unfurling their leaves, and even though I had rock mulch direct beneath them, all leaves were singed by the heat and the trees died again. The blackberries, of course, perished in the same fire.

The third spring I replanted once again, protecting them again with wire cages, and this time keeping the grass mowed around them. This time for three years they survived, with the only casualty recorded as a singed west half of a tree that was too close (within ten feet) to the un-mowed border prairie. By their third year I hadn't seen any deer visitors in my direct yard for at least two years and I removed the fence wire from the peaches and cherries, which the deer seemed to leave alone anyway, and an experimental removal of wire around the biggest apple tree seemed to also be permissible. They're in their fourth summer now and at least the peaches and cherries are starting to bear decent harvests.

At the same time as I was learning to protect the fruit trees from the deer, they had also ventured through or over the electric fence I had placed around the vegetable garden to combat rabbit plagues (see the essay titled *Wrastlin With Rabbits*), and they were contentedly munching on the sweet corn as quickly as it came up. A little trick from a gardening book turned the tide on that one. That expert recommended spreading peanut butter on aluminum foil and folding it over the center of the electric wires here and there. Although it seemed to be a bit cruel to make the point of current contact on the innocent deer's tongue as it tried to lick the peanut butter, one good ZAP and the deer were trained to keep away from the electric fence.

I thought I was fortunate that the deer had never chanced to bother the ornamental trees in the larger yard since the house was built, but I didn't really know why. Was it proximity to the house? Was it because they had to wander across the yard more exposed on the hill while the orchard meanders down the sides of a gully that offers them some protection? Was it the presence or barking of the dog in her pen at the corner of the house (she is normally quiet, but occasionally spends hours continually barking at some night creature or constellation that has offended her). But one night in late March last year I was considering a small horsechestnut (*Aesculus carnea* 'Briottii') placed in the middle of the back yard that I had just considered big enough to remove the protective fencing from the previous fall, and I was looking at the fat leaf buds (about an inch long and a half-inch wide) and thinking, "I bet those look appetizing to the critters, maybe I should replace the fence just in case." I didn't of course. The next morning, sure enough, the buds on the east half of the tree were nipped clean. The following morning, the other side of the tree was bare. I replaced the wire cage, where it remains today, muttering once again about the darned deer, but knowing who was really at fault (me). In the case of the horsechestnut, though, the deer ultimately did me a favor. It was the year of The Freeze and if the tree had made it into The Freeze with its leaves intact, I'm sure it would have killed it. As it was, the tree leafed out again about two weeks later, skipping over the critical temperature lows and although it didn't grow much that year, it survived to do well this year.

Interestingly enough, the deer have always seemed to leave my roses alone, despite the curses and lamentations on that subject from the East Coast gardeners. I had surmised that maybe Eastern deer are more cultured than our poorer prairie relatives and they only eat the most high-brow plants in the east. But last weekend I bought a new own-root hybrid tea rose in bud named 'Hot Cocoa' and planted it on Sunday in the formal rose bed. On Monday morning, it was just a series of stems with little deer footprints all around. Sometimes, I think I should just make a cement statue garden but the deer would probably just lick the statues into featureless lumps trying to get at the salt in the cement.

Of Lawns

I long ago opted for Buffalograss as the immediate lawn around our current rural prairie home and I am fully satisfied with maintaining the remainder of my lawn by trimming the native prairie grass. In fact, I was complimented the other day on my ecological bent of mind when I mentioned that most of my "yard" is merely mown tallgrass prairie, big bluestem, Indian grass, forbs, and all. This compliment came from one of the docents of the Konza Prairie preserve, an 8000 acre tall-grass research preserve complete with wandering buffalo and spring prairie fires that lies immediately south of Manhattan, Kansas. The complimenter perfectly fit your minds-eye image of one of those scholarly middle-aged or older women who serve as docents and volunteers at Museums and in society organizations all around the world. It may help to visualize her by picturing your third-grade teacher who put the fear of God into you if the connections on your cursive were slightly above or below the lines. She is one of those fit and intelligent members of the community in whose presence I immediately sit up straight, swallow my gum, and comb my hair. She's one of those individuals who become occasionally wild-eyed and rock society by some hopeless pursuit like getting women the vote or abolishing the sale of corn spirits. In my Master Gardener class, she served as the proponent for anything organically raised or xeriscaped. I did not disillusion her from her admiration by further admitting that I mow native prairie because I am essentially at depth a lazy soul, not one enlightened with the fires of abolition and progress. Nay, in fact I feel forever damned by cementing my image as an upstanding forward-thinking liberal ecologist through providing her with a catalog from High Country Gardens (highcountrygardens. com), a wonderful commercial nursery of Western native plants that provides both unique and well-grown plants for the gardener with xeriscapically-inclined intentions.

In point of fact, regarding lawns my sympathies lie more towards those of Michael Pollan's father. Pollan, one of my favorite garden writers, wrote in his book, *Second Nature,* that his urban father rebelled against his neighbors, the national suburban obsession with what he terms the "tyranny of the lawn" and coincidentally a father-in-law deeply steeped in love of the soil, by letting the lawn go completely unmown and wild one summer. I can empathize completely with the senior Pollan's response to the notes in the mailbox from angry neighbors, which was, according to Michael, to crank up the lawnmower, mow his initials in the untidy lawn, and put it back up for the rest of the summer. I won't attempt here to try and cloak myself and my lawnscaping motives in a deep philosophical dialogue regarding the history of the park system proposed by Capability Brown or the development of the suburban globe-circling lawn that the '50's culture made ubiquitous. I've read numerous learned texts analyzing just such societal movements and although I understand and keep my own council about it, my innate laziness defines my lawn. I've seen Central Park and, apologies to all New Yorkers, I'm not impressed with it. In the end, it's just a big wooded park with lots of ponds and stones, remarkable only in its size and location. That fact does not, however, take away from my admiration for New Yorkers as the American home front and first responders of the fight against terrorism.

I started out in our first suburban home with the best of lawn intentions. We moved into that house in late June towards the end of a ten-year drought in Kansas, a brand new house in a new addition on a

60X100 foot lot completely typical of modern housing developments. By which I mean that what stood for soil after the contractor removed the topsoil was the subsoil of the native prairie, a clay of consistency sufficient to make pots and whose fertility, if such a word can be used in relation to it, was lessened by the various large trucks and bulldozers that mixed it and molded it into large dry compacted clods extending down several feet. Visualize a brown concrete lot with a load of dry but muddy gravel deposited on it and you'll get the proper picture and consistency of the soil. But I was not totally naïve, no, not me, the wise descendent of generations of farmers. I made it a condition of the sale that the developer established a lawn in the month between our purchase in May and our arrival in late June. The developer, of course, proceeded with best low-cost intentions to get some mixed bluegrass and tall fescue to be established between the native weeds that sprung up instantly and uninvited, the latter being better suited to the drought conditions prevalent that summer. We arrived to the new house, our first "owned" home with its somewhat scraggly, somewhat patchy and somewhat green lawn and I proceeded to engage immediately in the suburban "one-up-man-ship" of who has the best lawn. I quickly found that a previously established neighbor was one of those older fiendish lawn veterans who have met the enemy and conquered it. Next to my drought-stricken weed patch was a beautifully manicured and edged lawn. To make the story short, if he could do it, I reasoned, then so could I. I proceeded over the next few years to fertilize and mow, aerate and mow, fertilize and mow, water and mow, power-slice and mow, amend the soil, reseed, fertilize and mow. And every week I'd do it all over again. I did this all with my own back, aided by my first purchased mower, an impressively engineered, powerfully driven mower purchased through mail-order. I knew from the beginning that my lawn was too small to justify purchasing a riding mower, or at least too small to keep me from being deeply embarrassed as I mowed with it, and I wasn't about to push up and down the slopes of the lawn with a mere Sears push-mower, so I went high-tech. My mower had an aluminum deck, front-wheel power drive, a mulching blade, a five HP state-of-the art motor and it was to put it kindly, a monstrosity. I paid extra for the optional grass bag, to gather the clippings. Of course, the power drive worked for approximately two weeks, leaving me nine years to push up and down the hills a lawnmower which was approximately four times heavier than average.

I learned several lessons in that first lawn. First, never let someone else plant your lawn for you as that someone else really doesn't care how well graded it will be or how good the soil is at the beginning. Second, always plant a single variety of grass because that way when it's mowed it stays looking mowed. If it's mixed, it will always look mixed with some parts growing faster than others and with natural selection choosing different varieties in different areas over time. Third, never get into a one-upmanship lawn war with your neighbor. Both of you will end just up older and more tired because of it.

After years of labor, though, there finally came a day when it was all worth it. One day, during a visit from my parents, my father surveyed my lawn and the neighbor's lawn, and in one of those brief instants so cherished and desired by sons down through time, he said something like "I think you've got your neighbor beat out for best lawn. He probably wishes you hadn't moved in next door to make him look bad." I think that's what I heard. Or maybe he said "Your neighbor's yard looks a little brown." Anyway, it was a great moment.

A Perfect Year

According to the optimist, the worst years are always followed by the best, and there is something to be said for optimism in the midst of despair. This year is indeed, so far at least, the perfect year for our gardens. Following the spring freeze and December ice storm from hell of last year, we needed it. And the plants needed it. We had a long, slow spring, warming up the air and soil both gradually and by some miracle, not accompanied by a hard freeze after mid-March. After last year's experience, I planted late, holding my breath as each week without frost went by until we were well past the last-frost dates. But nothing was frost damaged and everything germinated with gusto.

In contrast to the usual Kansas weather, it has rained frequently enough to get by the entire summer without any supplemental water anywhere in my garden. Now admittedly, my beds are well-mulched and getting deeper in mulch all the time, but steady rains have pelted us all through April to June. It got a little drier in July, but in the first week in August, just as I was contemplating hauling out the hoses, came a rain of five inches in twenty-four hours, resoaking the soil to great depths and leaving the perennials sighing in relief. But most importantly, the summer has been cooler than normal. I counted only three days where my outdoor thermometer hit 100°F or more, and only three or four weeks where it was in the nineties most of the time. August came, usually the hottest weather, and it stayed cooler and calmer than normal. And now, in mid-September, fall is coming gradually closer, the nights a little cooler each night, the days a little shorter, and again, the rain is coming. This is the first year that I can remember that I never stopped planting in my garden. I even planted a tree in early August. And the plant growth! I had bumper crops of blackberries, cherries, and peaches. Ornamental grasses grew to record heights. I lost not a single new plant to drought or heat during this summer, an unusual occurrence for me.

The pessimist, though, would tell you it was a lousy year for gardening. Over the entire county, people were bemoaning the poor tomato crop. The tomatoes, thriving as they do in hot and dry weather, were stunted everywhere in the Flint Hills and put out poor crops. Grapes, likewise needing hot weather, succumbed to fungus and produced half-hearted bunches of rotting grapes. Muskmelons and watermelons sat for weeks without growing or maturing. My rose garden sat in cool, saturated soggy clay all summer and the new roses either struggled all summer or drowned out.

I'll take all that, though, instead of late freezes, summer droughts, and ice storms.

Ex-Farm-Boy gardeners

Entire books and television shows have addressed from different venues the sometimes complex question of why we garden. I'm somewhat amused that ours is one of the first generations to probably even need to ask the question. Certainly the necessity for flower gardens has perhaps always been more perplexing, but for every generation up to these past few, the necessity to grow food and fruit in order to live was a given. Yes, there were a few elite who had others grow food for them and there was some division of labor for food production likely in the earliest cultures, but most of the Imperial Romans or the Frenchmen who fought for Joan of Arc could lay down their swords in one moment and correctly wield a hoe in the next. They didn't need to ask why, they needed to eat. The movement from the agricultural-based economy to industry over the past couple of centuries is changing our pattern of life, and I'm unconvinced it's for the better.

Most gardeners are quite able to articulate why we garden or at least supply some various reasons towards it. An astrologer might say I garden because I'm a Taurus, the earthy Bull. A psychiatrist might tell me I garden for peace and relaxation. I could tell you that I like to see things grow, or that I like to see unusual flowers, or that I feel good when friends tell me the garden looks nice. But primarily, I think I garden simply because it's in my soul and in my DNA. If the entire universe was myself and a plot of land, I'd still garden because that's the way it has to be.

My father and mother were raised on a farm, both my grandfathers and both grandmothers farmed, and likely their grandfathers for many German generations before them. I grew up on a farm and learned the rhythms of the seasons and soils at my father's and grandfather's knees. We moved from town to city when I was three years old. My father didn't actually farm the land in terms of sitting continually on a tractor. His was a generation that was starting to earn a living providing other products for civilization, but he brought us to live on one and my maternal grandfather actually farmed the ground, as he did several hundred other acres in the immediate neighborhood. And I was one of the lucky boys in my generation who still had the joys of acres of adventures outside their back doors.

From the age of three I learned to rise early and accompany an indulgent grandfather out to check cattle, rain or shine, snow or sleet. I can't fathom now why my mother would ever rise to dress me or allow me to be roused early in the dawn, this mother who was usually only partly functional before her morning coffee, but she did.

As I grew, my play time was interrupted more and more with the necessity and the abilities to do chores. As a result, my view of gardens as a teenager was from either somewhat grudgingly behind the handles of a tiller or aboard a lawnmower or with a hoe in my hands. And although I'm sure I grumbled and procrastinated, I really didn't mind. It was expected. I learned to paint fence, to hoe, to till the vegetable garden, and as I grew older, to take care of cattle and electric fences and occasionally to disc or cultivate when my grandfather fell behind the season's work. And I helped my father with the flower beds around the house although I couldn't fathom for an instant why he put so much time into merely growing flowers. My father and I had a good relationship with plenty of time devoted by a busy father to my attention, but that relationship had never extended to discussions of the "why?" of gardening. Truthfully, as common for men of our generations, we didn't talk much at all about philosophy or motivations when I was young. We grew food to have fresh food on the table. We did the things we did for the garden in order to bring the food to harvest. I never questioned and he never explained. My father planted annuals and trimmed shrubs every year, but my only speculation as to why he did it was that he wanted the house to look nice. And indeed, that may have been at least part of the motivation, but most of the other fathers I knew didn't indulge in beautification of the grounds, they were either in the fields or lived in town with houses landscaped in classic mustache form. I even remember thinking it was a strange and amusing thing for a father to do, surprising at a time when the father's of most of my friends spent little time in the yard or in house maintenance.

I also learned from my youth on the farm that farming for a living was an iffy thing, and by example that my father's manufacturing career provided surer income and extra income that would support the farm. My hard-working father's success also ultimately provided me with the freedom to choose my path and career, to choose an easier, if not necessarily better, life. I cast away the life of the land and hard toil and chose the way of the mind and science.

For too many generations, gardeners have received their horticultural educations subconsciously and sometimes by osmosis from our parents and grandparents. Sometimes we garden by habit. Sometimes we garden by fable ("Plant corn when oak leaves are as big as a squirrel's ear). Sometimes we get lucky. The paradigm shift of the new age is that lots of knowledge handed down in apprenticeship from generation to generation now has to be learned from books. If I've got any lesson to teach, it is that we must, we must, we HAVE to learn as gardeners to pass on to our children the really important knowledge consciously instead of expecting them to just somehow miraculously get it.

And for years, in college, I didn't think about growing plants. Sure, I was eventually in veterinary school and that implied some thought about farm animals and agriculture, but I had no urge to grow anything more fulfilling than a strawberry begonia briefly in the dorm room (it was the Seventies after all). I never believed I'd follow my father and do something as time-consuming and unrewarding as to plant a flower bed.

And yet there came a time when we purchased our first home, a brand new suburban home with bare ground, and no sooner did the ink get dry on the contract then I rushed out to buy a rose bush. I don't know why, but I knew I simply needed to. It was incredibly fulfilling. And then I planted more roses. And then I went from roses down the rabbit hole into full-fledged gardening obsession. I don't even remember now why I thought it was odd that my father gardened.

The point of the preceding indulgence in relating personal history is to convince you now that I don't believe I'm unique. I'm betting that there are literally thousands, if not millions of men in their forties who are former farm-boys and who garden today because it's actually true that you "can take the boy out of the farm but you can't get the farm out of the boy." We are lost boys, adrift on a service economy, with our minds on the earth. We garden for no other reason than that we need to garden. Some choose to make carefully weeded vegetable gardens, others to breed new daylilies. Some choose to grow giant pumpkins, others to obsess over the most tiny and rare plants in a backyard rock garden. But all of us are happiest with dirt under our fingernails and green in our vision.

Midden Misery

One unique creature to vex Kansas gardeners is the pack rat, also known as the Eastern Woodrat (*Neotoma floridana*). While they supposedly exist in my native Hoosier state, I do not recall ever seeing them or their homes. They were, at the least, not nearly as prevalent or as irritating as they are in Kansas. When we first moved onto the prairie, I had wondered what caused the piles of sticks that seemed to occur mostly at the base of the Eastern Red Cedars (*Juniperus virginiana*) or along old stone fences at the wood edges. These piles of sticks turned out to be the dwellings, or "middens," of pack rats. I could not see any indications of animal activity around the middens and didn't know what or who was piling up the twigs, but early on I noticed that when the piles against the tree trunks were ignited by the prairie fires, they'd serve as kindling to burn the normally fire-resistant Cedars.

I didn't mind that so much as the Eastern Red Cedar is a pioneer plant in Kansas. The term "pioneer" as used here does not refer to it being brought along with the Westward advance of civilization into the heathen lands for reasons of nostalgia, it refers to the fact that the cedar is one of the first plants to colonize bare ground after it's disturbed, and indeed, in Kansas the cedars will take over a prairie in a short number of years if fire is suppressed. It's one of the main reasons the prairies are burned regularly in this area. Unburned fields are thick and impenetrable in as few as three years with cedar seedlings.

I didn't realize the middens were pack rat condos until several years after living here. I did know that I had some kind of rodent stealing the dog's dry food and dried feces at night and moving these tidbits into the nearby rock wall landscaping. I once had six new own-root rose starts stored on my work bench in the garage in the early spring and shortly before the weather warmed enough to plant them, I went out one morning to find the pots bare with the canes clipped off at soil level, effectively wasting a $100 mail order. I knew that was a rodent too but didn't imagine anything more potent than a common mouse. And the following fall I noticed that at the southern edge of a large firethorn (*Pyracantha coccinea* 'Lowboy') there was a worn trail in the mulch leading under the bush, a trail that I assumed to be lagomorphic in origin and thought was a cute little hiding place for rabbits.

Sometime in the winter after the trail appeared, as the semi-evergreen firethorn thinned its leaves, I realized that at the center of the bush was a large nest of twigs, which upon research I realized was a real live pack rat nest. The same winter, another chummier or at least less fearful pack rat built a nice nest in my tool cabinet in the garage, coming and going through a little hole in the garage door seal that the builders had thoughtfully placed in order to allow their cords to extend out the door with the door down. In fact, the presence of urine areas and droppings in the garage soon made it clear that it was the center for the regional pack rat social club. Something had to change.

At the risk of some personal peril, I removed the midden in the garage cabinet with some concern that one of the little fur balls would find my jeans a convenient escape spot. I didn't want to make the same spectacle as my grandfather did one time in the hay loft when a mouse ran up his overalls and he spontaneously and instantly stripped before my young presence all the while spewing a cloud of words I had never before heard. Luckily, I accomplished the removal of the nest without incident. The pyracantha was a different matter altogether, though. I couldn't fathom being able to disassemble the midden from the center of that thorny shrub, so I cut the branches short to clear room away from neighboring plants and then lit the pile on fire with the aid of a few gallons of gasoline, all the while spraying neighboring plants with water to protect them as much as possible. I'd like to think I revenged my pyracantha by the death of a couple pack rats, but I never did find the slightest remnant of skeletal remains.

As rodents go, pack rats do have some redeeming qualities. They do have large dark eyes that are somewhat attractive, and at least they have the decency to cloth their tails in fur instead of leaving them scaly and naked. Their real redeeming value to society however, lies in their middens. Pack rats bring back all sorts of objects into their middens, anything shiny in particular, and these middens are often placed in dry protected areas and thus may survive intact for thousands of years. The pack rats improve on the structural integrity of the middens by urinating in it, cementing the midden together by crystals as the urine dries. Archaeologists have found these middens are a treasure trove for reconstructing the climate and vegetation of the area. Middens are abandoned after periods of time shorter than a few decades, leaving uncontaminated "time capsules." They are valuable enough to be better than pollen records as a method of study in areas they are available. The source of the large logs used by the Anasazi in treeless Chaco Canyon was determined to be local by the finding of pinyon needles in nearby middens, proof that the pines had grown there at the time (those middens were radiocarbon dated to over 1000 years old). In Kansas at a former mission school for Shawnee Indian children, archaeologists have retrieved eighty man-made artifacts dating from the mid-1800's from a midden that was discovered in 1983 in the ceiling of a building built in 1838. These included a handmade cloth doll and a child-sized set of dishes.

I think I'll try to keep the pack rats at bay here at home though, and create my own time capsules when and if I ever get the urge, although their permanence might be questioned since I don't plan to add urine as a building block. Right now we've worked out a truce where I allow the pack rat nests to be built in the woods and old stone fence at the south property line and I carefully scrutinize the bushes in the garden periodically to be sure no middens are growing in their middles. I recently found another nest and two babies placed back into the same tool cabinet in the garage and destroyed it, which has left me with a fit of conscience over the fate of the little pack rat children. On occasion I let the cats prowl around the house at night, though and that doesn't bother my conscience nearly as much. After all, no animal takes more and gives back less than a housecat and they need the opportunity to earn their feed somehow.

Purchased Tools

I'm definitely of a split nature regarding the availability and quality of modern gardening tools. On the one hand I'm mostly a traditionalist, revering most the tools that have sustained gardeners down through the ages. On the other, I'm not above trying out a new toy, with the result that my gardening cabinet and garage are lined with dozens of less-than-useful items that are held in disdain. The gardening tools of today are not the tools of our grandfathers, and in some instances that is a good thing, but usually the new ones are not an improvement on generations of experience.

When you're selecting gardening tools, in general it's best to avoid anything proclaimed as the newest boon to gardening. Believe me, if a whirligig on the end of a stick was really the best thing for pulling weeds since sliced bread, the Greeks or Romans would have invented it. If there's a need for it, the gardening serfs before us would have long ago thought about it, created it, modified it, and perfected it. After all, their profit motive was a full stomach instead of a handful of inked paper. The mowing scythe is a good example. A good curved mowing scythe, sharpened, set at the proper angle and with the handles appropriately placed, is the perfect combination of form to function, making effortless the cutting of swathes of tall grass. Another example is the rake. A simple functional bamboo or wire rake with a good long handle is much more satisfying and less harmful to the ears and environment than any motorized leaf-blower man ever made. Have you ever seen a frieze of a Roman centurion blowing the leaves off his patio with a motorized blower? I thought not and that's because it's not either a desirable or necessary improvement to the basic rake since it was invented.

It's also best to run screaming from any classic gardening tool that has been redesigned to be "ergonomic." For the most part, "ergonomically-designed" designates a tool that has been made in a strange shape, must be therefore held in an awkward manner, and whose price has been jacked up to pay for the advertising, all so you'll think it's a better tool. Ergonomic tools are designed, according to the Internet, "to maximize productivity by minimizing operator fatigue and discomfort." To my mind, therefore, the best ergonomic tool would be a paid servant, which is unfortunately out of my price range along with most of the other high-end ergonomic tools. Anything less than having someone else do the work and ergonomic simply means that an engineer has designed it, leaving it, as engineers are wont to do, in as awkward and nonfunctional a condition as possible.

Do you really think that ancient gardeners, who spent far more time with a hoe, shovel, or trowel in their hands then we do, would have not over the years evolved their tools into the perfect functional forms? Or that, despite whether our tools are designed in modern ergonomic fashion, we shouldn't expect a bit of soreness at the end of a day or a few new calluses on our palms? No, in truth, we view the "old" tools less useful because we've forgotten how to properly use them. We've forgotten how to hold rake and hoe to prevent sore backs or arms. Because of cost or availability, we fail to buy a long enough handle to prevent bending over while working or we buy a shovel with too long a handle and therefore strain our backs lifting. We jump on our shovels and bruise our insoles instead of learning to push it into the ground with a firm boot. And avoiding calluses on our hands isn't possible even with ergonomic design. Calluses are simply nature's way of both toughening the gardener and making the gardener more ergonomic for the tool. Don't shape the tool, nature tells us, shape the gardener.

What the general market lacks are gardening tools that come made of lasting materials and properly sharpened. The lasting materials issue can be overcome by careful search of multitudes of stores until the proper tools are located and by willingness to pay out the nose for quality. Forget about anything which incorporates plastic into its construction. Garden tools made of plastic should be viewed as disposable. They crack or break in the cold, warp in the heat, blanch and become brittle in the sun, or just plain wear out faster. I currently have nothing left in my garden space that's made of plastic from the traveling sprinklers to the rakes with the exception of a plastic wheelbarrow which has a cracked bottom and should be replaced. Solid steel construction, strong wood handles, and firm connections are the ticket to true convenience. It goes without saying that most handles on good tools should be made of ash or walnut or some other similarly durable hardwood. In some cases, fiberglass handles are lighter and are an improvement on wood handles, but they often vibrate more than the wood, leading to repetitive injury. Handles of plastic or softer woods are fleeting and in some cases dangerous to use.

What isn't possible in modern commerce is to find a tool which is already properly sharpened. Busy lawyers and occupational safety experts have resulted in a market devoid of any tools that are sold in a condition sharp enough to be useful. News flash for tool manufacturers; most gardening tools have some sort of cutting function. Further news flash; a hoe should be sharp. Almost every gardener I know buys their Dutch or common garden hoe, which comes with a nice blunted edge and immediately goes to hacking at the ground with it. I was thirty-five years old before I discovered that weeding with a hoe was best practiced by pull-cutting weeds off at or just beneath the surface and that a sharp cavex hoe was the best hoe to perform this action. Suddenly I found myself enjoying a previously avoided chore, and my plants were benefitting from the increased attention. It is an epiphany to realize that you don't flail repeatedly at the ground to hoe it. The cavex hoe is an old design with a curved blade form best exhibited today as the Razorback series of hoes. Avoid the modern "hula" or scuffling hoes. They don't really work better than a cavex hoe and they also are marketed in dull as a rock form and are made of inferior steel to boot.

Children and Gardening

A common urge, as we ponder the end to this life, is that we want to leave more behind to our children, more lessons we wish we'd taught, and more paths to follow for the betterment of the lives of our descendents. We leave unfortunately little of ourselves behind, fleeting memories in the thoughts of loved ones which will dim and finally die as the next generation follows us. And the lessons our children learn are often not the best lessons we would have chosen if we really knew what we were going to pass down. Our human failings may result in poor choices, and in those choices, the lessons passed on may be poorer than we'd hoped.

Gardeners, though, have an advantage in this quest to care for our loved ones after we're gone. I believe that the gardener can pass on a single lesson that will serve his or her children for the rest of their lives. We can pass on the spark of nature, the urge to garden, and latent though it may be in a teenager, whatever else happens we can be sure that it will start to burn strongly when it's most needed, and that it will continue to teach them new ways to face life as time passes.

I was thinking today of all the lessons of life we are taught as we garden. If you are of a mind that the knowledge learned in gardening extends only to the action of sun and water, of caring for the soil to nurture plants, and of plant forms too numerous to count, then you have sorely missed the real lessons of a garden. You've missed the program and Acts I and II of the great play.

It's easy to say that we and later our children learn the importance of patience from gardening. The two members of the Instant Gratification Generation that are part of my family will badly need those lessons of patience as they age. The garden can teach them that growth, plant or otherwise, occurs only at its own pace, and it can't be hurried with artificial fertilizer or curses or worrying. It teaches that the only antidote to loss is to replant and start again. It can instruct the young that surprises are a moment to be savored, and that planning doesn't always result in the expected outcome. To a parent, the garden teaches that the oak tree will take years to reach its full, glorious potential, and that although the rose is beautiful, it, like our children it opens only a petal at a time. Change and growth in the garden occurs only at its own pace, not at the pace the gardener desires. It becomes apparent only after much study that only the addition of more sunlight will increase the rate of plant growth, just as more sunlight and happiness makes our own growth stronger and healthier. The garden also teaches that a little rain also helps growth. Those cold wet days when our feet are stuck in mud are as necessary as the sunny days to give us rest and time to gather ourselves for the next spurt. Yes, a cloudy day can set us back a bit, but it also makes us appreciate the sunshine all the more.

I can see the seeds of the gardening gene in my own children already, latent though it may be. Up to this point, they've mostly been reluctant participants at best. My long-suffering daughter, a precocious four-year-old at the time, once recognized that we were pulling up to a garden center and exclaimed "not more roses!" In her teens now, she has a few garden events she likes to be made aware of when they are happening, like the planting of bulbs and the harvest of pumpkins, but for the most part, the garden merely exists in her background right now. My erstwhile hippie son, now nearing the milestone of twenty-one years old, also is showing horticultural interests, primarily in indoor aeroponics and hydroponics. If I'm somewhat suspicious of exactly what crop(s) he might be cultivating, it is still another indication that the gardening genes can't be denied.

Meconopsisless

I know where my limits with blue flowers lie, primarily because I've proved it over and over. If all gardening is one long regret, then my biggest regret is that I cannot grow the fabled plant that is the pinnacle within the blue spectrum. I describe it as the pinnacle not because I have grown and bloomed it, but because I have lusted after it, dreamed of it, and done everything possible to grow it short of packing up and moving to British Columbia. There is but one perfect blue flower in the world according to all sources, and that is the blue *Himalayan Poppy* (Meconopsis betonicifolia) and I agree. It (sob) will simply not grow in Kansas, either indoors or outdoors in my experience. I am regretfully meconopsisless, doomed like Eleanor Perenyi to want to "give anything for a glimpse of it, even in somebody else's garden." I've ordered numerous small doomed specimens, planted at all times of the year, outside, in the ground and in containers, in shade and in sun. Some of them actually survive in wretched condition two weeks before shriveling to brown mush, but none ever showed the slightest inclination to make my joy complete by blooming. I first became aware of Meconopsis pictured in magazines and books, always colored magnificently with what I suspected was artificial printing enhancement. Then once, on business in Vancouver and playing hooky at the VanDusen Botanical Garden, I rounded a bend in the path and stood as dumbstruck as I would have if blue aliens had landed in my backyard. It luminesced, it shone, it shouted, it was BLUE! So perfectly, daintily, calmingly, restfully blue. For others who read about but have not seen this cerulean debutante, I must fess up that the magazine pictures do not do it justice any more than a 2X3 Polaroid snapshot of the Acropolis does justice to the beauty of that ancient structure.

Being forever meconopisless might be vaguely tolerable if not for the constant needling (often manifested as faux sympathy) from authors who can grow the plant and worse, advice from more boastful authors that the Meconopis is simple, SIMPLE I tell you, to grow. Wayne Winterrowd gives me no quarter to feel better about my failure, finishing his chapter on the Meconopis in Jamaica Kincaid's *My Favorite Plant* with the words; "How dreadfully sad I am for other gardener's who cannot have them." As an added insult, he relates receiving Meconopsis as a gift, whose value was not known until it bloomed. Wayne, if you can't appreciate the miracle you've been given, just kindly send me a bit of your ground and an enclosure containing your climate and I'll be glad to worship it for you. In fact, I think Ms. Perenyi has it wrong; I'm not normally vindictive, but if I can't grow it, I don't want to see it in someone else's garden either. Winterrowd lists a number of cultivars of Meconopis betonicifolia and Meconopis grandis, none of which I can grow. I know that others of the genus, particularly Meconopis cambrica are perhaps easier to grow and possible here, but who really wants a yellow poppy as the weak cousin to the prince of poppies? But for the wind and drought and sun and prairie fires and critters here, I'm sure I could get the blue poppy to grow, and I'm sure that someday I'll try again. I have contemplated moving to a Meconopsis-friendly climate and in that case, I believe I would forego all other garden plants and simply have bed after bed of perfect blue poppies. Take note, all you hybridizers trying to add blue pigment to the rose. Focus your efforts instead on making Meconopsis as hardy as Oriental poppies and your fortune is made. Lucifer, if you ever would like to bargain for my soul, come bearing Meconopsis.

And by the way, it's mec-on-op-sis, not me-con-o-psis.

Time to Rest

I sat down in the garden yesterday, for the first time this past summer, choosing for my sojourn the cement bench in the middle of my rose garden. It was a dreary Saturday, filled with drizzle and clouds, and I'd finished the planned garden chores, the new 'Morning Light' (*Miscanthus sinensis*) grass clump planted, the volunteer Cottonwood tree moved, and the patio swept. And so, at the end of the chores, I plopped down and experienced the quiet peacefulness, broken only by the distant sound of the highway and the more distant cheers of the Kansas State University crowd at the football stadium. The fall rampant bloom of the roses filled the immediate vicinity with color and from fifty feet away came the achingly glorious scent of the Sweet Autumn Clematis (*Clematis paniculata*). I sat for a moment and gazed at the figure of a statue across the garden and I didn't think, I tried to just be.

Do as I say, not as I do; Sit in your garden! I unfortunately spend little time sitting in my own garden. As it is a young garden, I'm always in the middle of an expansion or plan that allows me little time for enjoyment of the growth I've wrought. There's always something to do, another bed to prepare, the compost to turn, or a plant to divide. And the new plants, always planting new plants. I'm a serial impulse plant buyer and I confess that I buy without thought to where it will be placed. For me, gardens are the plants. Excuses, Excuses.

What we miss by not enjoying our own gardens! After all, who do we garden, for, anyway? In my case, my garden is surely not created for enjoyment for anyone else; there are no public tours of my garden (at least not yet), only two of my neighbors have anything approaching a decent view of my garden, and my wife and teenage daughter rarely venture out into it. And in fact, when the latter do come out, they tend to suggest things that make me think that the garden is definitely not meeting their expectations such as my wife's comments that I have too many pink roses and not enough other colors, or my daughter's comment on the new area covered with paving stones (It's Tacky!). No, I, as most gardeners, garden primarily for my own enjoyment, an entertainment which seems so far to consist mostly of doing, rather than savoring. I must do better about being in my garden rather than working my garden.

In my own garden, I don't often sit down for a number of reasons. One is certainly a current lack of comfortable places to sit because there are only two benches, one against the house which really serves as cover over a gas line (wouldn't want to be sitting there when the line leaked!) and the other in the rose garden. Both benches are concrete, without back support, and without shade to boot. They are met to be seen, not really to be sat on, although changing their placement might facilitate them being used in the manner for which they were designed. In my defense, even shade might not help get me to sit on one of them in the sweltering July heat in Kansas. I also can't often sit in the garden because of the list; the chore list which I set out to accomplish when I have time to garden. Just getting through that list provides all the feeling of accomplishment and satisfaction as an hour's rest would. But I'd suspect the main reason I don't sit down to enjoy my garden is that I haven't learned to do so. I haven't made a habit of that which I know would otherwise be good for my mental and physical health. Why, in fact, are most habits bad for those latter two most important things of life?

I have been slowly making movement towards that goal, although part of that movement is only in my mind. Just this year, I made a short tunnel of lattice that is now beginning to be covered with wisteria from both sides. It has provided a nice shady spot to stand and swelter in as I approach sunstroke on the hottest summer days and I take advantage of it for thirty second periods as I pass by. It would possibly work better as a resting place, if, as suggested by my wife, I were to string a hammock between the sides, but then I couldn't run the lawnmower through it easily. Maybe next year. Along those lines She Who Must Be Obeyed has suggested that a gazebo might be a nice structure to take the place of the unused trampoline which remains as an eyesore in the garden from the days when my children were children. And I'm already picturing it; a gazebo with a roofed top, with a hammock strung in the middle to read and sleep in. So to properly sit and enjoy my garden I'll take on yet another project soon. Perhaps it's no accident that those gardeners that seem to rest most in their gardens are the older generation and they rest because the aches and creaks of their bones would conflict with the quiet of the garden.

In my experience, the gardener will be encouraged to sit and take in the garden in one of two ways. The first is to employ a vast entourage of personnel who do the actual work of gardening, leaving the gardener, if such one can be called, to enjoy the fruits of their money, if not their labor. That first option has been out of the budget of many gardeners, including myself, since early in the twentieth century, serving as more proof that there has been a slow decline in living conditions despite technologic advances over the past century. The second option is to provide as many perfect sitting places as possible within the garden. In my opinion, perfect sitting places have three qualities; they must be placed so that as little undone work can be noticed as possible, they must offer protection from the elements and must, in particular, be shady, and finally, they must be comfortable enough to sit in that the weary gardener finds themselves unable to summon energy to move out of them. Ideally, a perfect sitting place is therefore a soft lounge chair placed high within a dense maple tree, something that is entirely lacking from most gardens.

I had just such a spot as a young boy, a nook cradled by stout limbs high in a Norway maple near home, and I spent entire summers reading there. It didn't have a lounge chair placed up high, but that was no drawback as young bodies don't require as much packing for comfort. And it provided the perfect cool, quiet setting to observe the comings and goings of farm life, including the efforts of my mother to find me when I hadn't been seen for a few hours at a time. Amazingly, she never did catch on that I was often mere feet above her head when I wasn't answering her call. Towards supper, a quick climb down and a flip off the lowest branch and I'd reenter the world invigorated by the combination of rest and the unpressured life of a child. I need that tree again now and hopefully one of the cottonwoods growing on the perimeter of my garden will supply it when I'm in my sixties and ready to sit down. I'd better start working on the chair hoist, though, since I won't be able to climb the tree by then.

Hybridizers and Nature's Colors

What's wrong with magenta, you ask? After all, the mere elimination of magenta from the garden color scheme decreases the possible choices of flowering plants by approximately 90%. Eleanor Perényi in *Green Thoughts*, writes that magenta is the original shade of most flowers. I admit that I find magenta, alone, a lovely color, which can mix well with the green of the foliage in some perennials. My problem comes with merging it with other plants in the garden. A blossom a little too pink on one side, a little too blue on the other and I feel like the social director at a Hatfield and McCoy wedding; I might find a place to temporarily put a cantankerous guest, but sooner or later the sneers and shoving will result in the appearance of guns.

One of my pet gardening peeves was piqued today when I received a Fall catalogue of a national plant company in the mail (which shall remain nameless since I'm about to criticize it and don't wish to be sued for libel). Why, pray tell, can't the plant hybridizers of the world leave well enough alone? Isn't it enough that they have gone out of their way to create white marigolds and are attempting to instill blue into the rose? Must they mess with all species till they are ruined beyond repair?

The particular item to start this rant is illustrated by a page entitled "Coneflower Extravaganza." Yes, you creators of hideous plants and gaudy catalogue spreads, you go ahead and duck your heads and try to hide. You know who you are and we know who you are. You've now started in on the plain coneflower and you're determined to ruin this prairie gem, aren't you?

I have a particular liking for coneflowers as they occur as natural forbs in the Kansas prairie and do very well in Kansas gardens in general. The naturally occurring coneflower species, *Echinacea purpurea,* raises its regal light pink petals and turns its brown face to the sun about mid to late June in my area, and I enjoy the display dotting the prairies very much, thank you. The pink of the native coneflower is just right, bright enough to be seen and stand out against the green grass, not too fluorescent or showy to grate on one's nerves.

I've been aware for a few years now that there is a seeming revolution in cultivars of Echinacea. I've tolerated without extreme rancor the selection of the true white coneflower 'White Swan', even though its display is inferior in the garden to the Shasta daisies which hold their petals up firmer and have their nice orange center to stand out. I've even taken a fancy to orange-brown 'Sundown' and grow several of the latter in my garden. But this Fall's catalogue pictures a number of cultivars I've rarely or never seen, and it's clear that somebody somewhere is trying to either make the coneflower into a Shasta Daisy (*Chrysanthemum sp.*), or, in another direction, trying to imitate their dear Auntie's pink fuzzy bathroom slippers. 'Razzmatazz' is the first Frankenstein creation to test the eye with its bright fuchsia-pink fuzzy center hiding the delicate but similarly hideously colored petals. 'Pink Double Delight' also seems to be an Echinacea in the process of trying to look like a Pepto-Bismol-colored carnation. 'Green Envy,' described as "totally different and nothing short of spectacular," is in fact a little short of spectacular in the illustration and is obviously for sale not because it will add anything of value to a given garden, but because somewhere over the rainbow, hybridizers have correctly surmised that some tasteless gardener will buy any flower colored lime-green. I'm not that envious and don't plan to grow 'Green Envy.' 'Sunrise,' labeled as being "a rare color in coneflowers," is in fact a light yellow or cream coneflower whose centers turn gold and help it to imitate a Shasta daisy. And heaven forbid I forget to see on another page 'After Midnight', a dwarf coneflower with rose-purple blooms, or 'Harvest Moon,' a gold colored Echinacea looking for all the world like a miniature sunflower.

Worse of all are two selections which take good taste further down the sewer. 'Coconut Lime' looks like the deformed 'Razzmatazz' in shape, yet it is pale lime green and is even described as the "green Razzmatazz." Talk about the child being uglier than the parents! And of course, there is a selection called 'Black Beauty' whose petals are dwarfed, leaving a black center on display for the pleasure of Gothic gardeners who wear black clothes and like black tulips and pea sticks in their gardens. I'm betting 'Black Beauty' disappears against the background when placed into the garden, thus showing the embarrassment of the plant itself as it tries to shrink into the background rather than display its strangeness to the rest of us.

I sometimes wonder why I get upset at such trivialities. After all, this is a catalogue which lists a new Coreopsis cultivar 'Jethro Tull.' Now, I'm of the age that I listened to the music of Jethro Tull when it was new, and I'm afraid I don't see the resemblance in a yellow flower, even if we are describing the petals as "fluted," whatever that is. And on the page after the Echinacea explosion, are two Shasta Daisies *(Leucanthemum superbum)* which look nothing like themselves. We are commanded by the catalogue to "grow this petite fringed beauty," the aborted daisy 'Gold Rush," who has an abundance of fluffy petals in three to four inch flowers on fourteen inch plants (another pet peeve of mine is giant flowers on dwarf plants which cause one to think the flowers are laying on the ground itself). And beside it is 'Sunny Side Up,' another dwarf Leucanthemum where the center is raised to look like it belongs on a cornflower. And still the catalogue goes on to the new Heucheras, with the chameleon 'Tiramisu' featured prominently. 'Tiramisu' goes through three phases of color, a tolerable peachy yellow in spring, a lime-green summer foliage, and then ends up looking for all the world like a pink and green Coleus in the fall. It should have stopped in the summer while it was ahead.

Wrastlin' with Rabbits

Helen Dillon, in her book *Down to Earth*, states that she has "always had a theory that a vegetable tastes particularly good served along with something that eats it; a pigeon with broccoli, rabbit with lettuce... and so on." I believe that my sweet wife, having been raised on a steady diet of rabbit and squirrel (contemplation of which explains a lot about her unswerving carnivorous nature), would agree wholeheartedly with Ms. Dillon. Now, myself, being a vegetarian, or more accurately a lacto-ovo-macrobiotics vegetarian since I consume mostly pasta and dairy, I pretty well leave the rabbits in my yard to proliferate freely as rabbits tend to do. And since I'm pretty sure that early spring iris and daylilies are the primary rabbit food around here, I don't intend to serve either to guests, figuring that even if they liked the rabbit, they probably wouldn't enjoy the daylilies, however edible some texts claim the latter to be.

The primary rabbit species present in this area of Kansas seems to be the Eastern Cottontail (*Sylvilagus floridanus*). These furry-tailed mammals are usually encountered near a resting shelter composed of a slight depression on the surface of the ground protected overhead by a canopy of grass or low shrub. Although my garden never seems to be without a few of them, brief research tells me the individuals are short-lived, with the average life-span approximately less than a year before they surrender to predator or disease. I assume the rabbits in my garden live in constant fear of the packs of coyotes that interrupt my slumber on clear fall nights, but they seem to be indifferent to the dogs and cats that live with us. I myself used to live in fear of the damage they could do to my garden, but find them harmless interlopers and companions now. I confess to being infatuated with the young that I occasionally find as orphaned survivors from prairie fires or as wayward escapees from the nest. These quiet, little, brown-eyed, and soft creatures are as compact as they are cuddly, and they sit quietly when held as if they don't believe we know they are there as long as they don't move. They do tremble in a most unsettling way when you hold them.

In truth, I have come full circle on the philosophy of live and let live with my Kansas rabbits. Early on, in the establishment of my garden, I blamed a number of vegetative losses rightfully on the rabbits and took action squarely to intimidate and repel the little floppy-eared invaders. I was encouraged when my first attempt at a vegetable garden on the prairie showed the promising sprouting of a couple of rows of early string beans, only to find one morning that the entire row had been wiped away down to stems. It's a sad sight, that straight row of little two-inch stems smack in the middle of the garden, and enough to turn a gardener into a raving, spitting creature bent on vengeance. I briefly considered using them as expendables for my newfound hobby of target practice, but ultimately decided that organic gardening practices did not call for return of the rabbits themselves to the compost pile. Instead, I quickly learned the value of an enclosure of electric fencing, with the bottom two wires spaced approximately two and four inches above the ground. That structure succeeded in shocking the rabbits into understanding my determination to keep them out of the garden and they acquiesced at once. For several subsequent years, I have been able to raise nice crops of lettuce and beans in the vegetable garden, although towards the end of each season I mysteriously lose a few cantaloupes and other melons to an invader that seems to be attracted to the musky sweetness within and which I believe to be either rabbits (which I still occasionally see within the demilitarized zone of the garden), or box turtles (which are rumored to like melons and which could conceivably be immune or grounded to the garden fence).

In the greater garden outside the fence, I lived in initial fear of the damage rabbits could heap upon me, but I have matured to believe that little actual mischief occurs. This past summer, for instance, I had no fewer than at least four permanent lagomorphic boarders in my garden, a fact that I confirmed by simultaneous visualization of all four from the back garden patio. Yet despite the sheer tonnage of rabbit meat grazing on my garden, I noticed only a few nibbles on early iris and daylily sprouts that I surmised as having been nipped by pairs of opposing buck-teeth. I somehow again refrained from taking aim and firing upon them when I found the iris nipped, and I'm now glad that I did not pull out the full-auto weaponry too quickly. Once spring was in full opulence, as the prairie grass and other plants greened up, I could not find any further damage and the iris and daylilies grew tall and bloomed on schedule. The rabbits, though, remained as tenants in the garden, living under several concealing shrubs including a *Juniper* 'Youngstown Andorra' that is a scant twenty feet from my bedroom window. As the summer wore on, they provided a fleeting sort of companionship to my garden forays, always freezing at my initial appearance in the garden as if they thought themselves invisible when only a few feet away, and then afterward bounding away when they realized they'd been spotted by the tall predator. When I stay concealed, watching them through the house windows, they primarily stay moving and visible in the close-cut open prairie grass, seemingly unafraid of the prairie hawks, taking a couple of hops here and a couple of nibbles there, always of the lawn. They never seem to enter the garden beds except for concealment and thus I both allow and protect their presence. A casual visitor to my garden would, in fact, believe that I have joined a religion whose deity has floppy ears as there are no fewer than five rabbit statues in my garden. Sometimes I wonder if the native rabbits look on my statues as an invitation, as the numbers of both statues and live rabbits seem to increase in the garden with each passing year.

The Seven Gardening Sins

The Seven Deadly Sins as listed by Pope Gregory the Great in the sixth century were created to instruct the heathen and bring them into the Christian fold, but also seem to have been created specifically for gardeners. For those uninitiated to Christian philosophy, the capital sins are listed as Pride, Envy, Anger, Sloth, Greed, Gluttony, and Lust, listed in increasing seriousness as they offended against love. Interesting that Pope Gregory chose to list them by such a criteria, which suggests that the presumably fat old friar was not unacquainted with the pleasures of the flesh. In researching the seven deadly sins, I was intrigued that they are also represented by colors, in like order as violet, green, red, light blue, yellow, orange, and blue, thus giving us the common language of turning "green with envy" or "red with anger", and that there are contrary or opposite virtues to the sins in order of humility, kindness, patience, diligence, charity, temperance, and chastity. Good grief, must the language of sin and virtue be so intricate? Can we not recognize our own sinful ways by the weight pulling on our own souls? Most all gardeners are pure enough of heart to recognize their own sinful ways in the garden, but although the sins may be self-explanatory, I'll expand on each separately in terms of how I see them apply to gardening.

First, I would propose that we reorder them in view of their increasing sinfulness in the garden thusly; wrath, envy, greed, pride, lust, gluttony, and sloth, the latter absolutely being the worst sin, if any are in fact, sins, because sloth in the garden in essence negates the garden and leaves only a wilderness. In fact, I think the first six mentioned should not be considered sinful, leaving sloth as the only possible real gardening sin. And, since the virtues are all still good for our gardens, I would ask, "is sin really possible in the garden?" Or, as long as we maintain a garden, are we sinless and still in Eden (excluding of course, the planting of purple barberry and orange daylilies).

Wrath, as a mortal gardening sin should be first and least important if we include it at all, because wrath is a normal part of gardening and I don't believe it is necessarily wicked at all. We rightly feel wrath in the garden when the rabbits chew on the new daylily shoots or the mice strip the bark off the winterized roses, and we should appropriately plot the demise of Satan's furry apprentices. As another example, it is right to feel wrath against the neighbor's Norway Maple tree that grows and shades a good half of our vegetable garden, let alone ignore the fact that its roots are stealing all the water from the ground. A final example, am I not within my rights to feel wrath towards the heavens that open up with golf-ball sized hail and strip the leaves from the lilies? If we can't feel wrath towards those who would destroy our gardens, then what good would we be to our garden?

Envy, Greed, and Lust, all have the same meaning as it pertains to the garden, and if sins they be, most gardeners are guilty. Can it really be wrong to envy our neighbor's ability to raise dahlias? I say, nay, envy is not a sin in the garden as it pushes us upwards towards better gardening practices. I envy those who can grow the Blue Himalayan Poppy, but that envy only serves to keep me purchasing more seedlings (good for capitalism), trying different ways to grow them (good for my education as a gardener), or buying more gardening magazines with advice about them (good for garden writers and editors). Is greed sinful if we want to collect samples of all the commercially-available Bourbon roses or is that just an example of the obsessive-compulsive disorder common to rosarians? And what if the third world war wiped out all other examples of Bourbons except those saved in that gardener's yard? Greed would have been a good thing, no? Is lust for that particular garden plant or pergola seen in the city park a sin? No, I say, lust would only be a gardening sin if we were to traipse off with the neighboring gardener's wife and rendezvous beneath said pergola. In short, Envy, Greed and Lust are all just byproducts of normal gardening that strive to make our gardens better and are only sinful if they actually lead us to destructive acts such as salting the neighbor's petunias so that ours would look better by comparison.

Pride as a sin? I believe it's self-evident that pride in the gardener would be a good aspect of gardening, leaving the gardener happy in his or her creation. Just think, without pride, there would be no local garden tours because we would have no desire to let others into our gardens. Anyway, in reality, any pride exhibited in our gardens is just allowed as a shining brief moment by the gardening gods before a massive hailstorm is sent to leave the garden drooping in tattered shambles along with the ego of the gardener.

Now in Gluttony I begin to see the first inkling that one of the original sins may also be evil for the garden, not for all gardens, but in some gardens. Some of the most beautiful gardens I've ever seen are also some of the most gluttonous, bountiful and overflowing with oodles of plants and statues, and vistas. We're taught by the organic movement that close planting, almost gluttonous planting, may suppress weeds and shade the ground to hold in moisture and all that may be good. But, in contrast, gluttony where it pertains to single-mindedness may not be good for the garden. If one were to purchase every plant one sees to the detriment of having no budget for a nice statue, or time to create a shady resting nook, then where would that leave the garden? It becomes only a wild, shapeless and order-less group of plants. If we can't quell our plant acquisitions long enough to eat, what becomes of the garden? A gardener could also exhibit gluttony by expanding territory for gardening; the Gardens of Versailles come to mind. Such a large formal garden, punctuated with immaculately coiffured topiary and carefully designed vistas, is quite beautiful only if one forgets that there are flowers in the world, and perhaps serfs who might need the land for sustenance.

It is Sloth that I really believe may be the only unequivocal sin in the garden. Perhaps it's just my Germanic heritage or the Puritan streak that tells me we're put on this earth to live, love, work, and die. Perhaps it's the fact that I've forgotten, in the midst of wife, children, job and gardening hobby, how I might sit and relax. But I must rail against Sloth in the garden. To allow Sloth is to allow corruption to invade our gardens. Sit back for a moment, and reflect on what must surround a slothful gardener. Defend the virtues of weeds, admire their strength and resourcefulness if you must, but never doubt that you would not want a garden full of them. Without Sloth's counterpart, Industriousness, the garden would fall to wild plants and wild creatures. There would be no choice between organic and inorganic, no battle between rabbit and vegetable farmer, no loss of species because meddling with nature by Man. Wait, what am I saying? Could it be that Sloth, in moderation, is good for the garden? If I let the milkweeds grow instead of steadfastly cutting them down, is my garden improved because the monarch caterpillar can live there? If I don't deadhead the roses, are the resulting plump orange-red hips of winter really a distraction from the beauty of the garden? Is it a Faustian bargain for our gardening souls if we choose, just once, to sit on the garden bench and smell the Autumn Clematis?

Putting the Dog Bowl Away

Among my many failings as a gardener, I must count my complete inability to cull an awkward, ugly, weak, or otherwise disappointing plant out of my garden. If you share this weakness, I encourage you to listen when I say that the prettiest gardens undoubtedly have the most ruthless gardeners. But I also know that you won't listen. It's the nature of the gardener to either be able to eliminate the plants who don't measure up or to struggle along with them hoping they'll grow up and mature from that ugly duckling to a beautiful swan.

My sister and I refer to the probably healthy trait of moving on as "putting the dog bowl away," a phrase coined from the actual actions of my mother. Mom has an uncanny ability to put unpleasurable experiences out of her consciousness, as once demonstrated when a house dog she was close to was killed by an automobile one winter day. Before my father and I could remove the still-warm body from the side of the road, Mom had cleaned and washed the dog bowls and put them up out of sight, hence the reference to "putting the dog bowl away." Needless to say, the rest of us have a secret family pact that if any of us are ever on life support, Mom won't be allowed near the equipment or electrical plugs in the hospital room.

I was reminded how commonly we fail as gardeners to do the unpleasant chores of plant selection by a radio show yesterday. Crossing Indiana, I came across a call-in show where one gardener mentioned she had just given up on her Japanese Stewartia (*Stewartia pseudocamellia*) and the host also agreed that the tree hadn't measured up to her expectations. If you look at a description of the Stewartia, say, the one by Marie Hofer on hgtv.com that describes it as one of the best small trees available with "lovely four season usefulness (bark color, flower, and fall foliage), you'd probably want to grow it as well and if it grows anywhere, it should grow in Southern Indiana where its requirements for temperature and acid soil are easily met. But here were two gardeners that had tried repeatedly in that region and failed with the plant. I, myself, haven't been enticed into a Stewartia yet and it's just as well that one hasn't appeared in a local nursery or I'd have already failed with it, adding it to the many that I just shouldn't have tried. I mean, other than that the descriptions say it doesn't tolerate wind or drought, prefers acid soils, and is extremely hard to establish, what would keep it from growing well here in Kansas?

I have plenty of horticultural examples that I persist in torturing and a sane person would wonder why I haven't yet pulled the plug on some of them. Consider that I continue to occasionally try to grow various azaleas and rhododendrons, trying different conditions each time, amending the soil, trying them in shade and sun, in raised beds and in swamps. I have overwintered exactly zero to date. Given the alkaline soil, it's small wonder that the poor things are doomed the minute I plunk down cash for them, but they are sold, for heaven's sake, at every nursery in a one hundred mile radius so they must grow here, right? I choose to ignore the fact that I've seen a mature specimen in only one garden in my area, grown in a woody river-bottom grove by a local nursery owner, and I'm watching carefully another at the Kansas State University gardens that has survived a second season. I suspect it's a conspiracy by local nurseries and box stores to sell what is essentially an expensive annual without actually pointing out what they're doing. Other species that I have tremendous trouble getting established are *Itea virginica* varieties such as 'Henry's Garnet' and *Clethra alnifolia*

'Ruby Spice'. Both seem to have required multiple attempts and careful attention to extra water to become established in my garden. But I keep trying them and have been successful once with 'Henry's Garnet', but not yet with 'Ruby Spice'. Hope springs eternal.

In my current garden are several plants that I simply don't like, but unless one demonstrates its desire to colonize neighboring areas, I wait and provide it a chance to prove itself to me. Take, for example, the caryopteris 'Snow Fairy' (*Caryopteris divaricata* 'Snow Fairy') growing prominently in the front of my hydrangea bed. I once chose it for the wonderful variegated foliage and I admit it has a very nice light blue flower. It was easy to establish and stands the full force of the Kansas sun well. In truth, however, the flowers come on late and their light color practically disappears against the foliage, and the plant itself dies back to the ground every winter here so it never provides any visual benefit to the garden until it reaches the two foot stage in late August. A similar unappealing plant to me is the red bamboo 'Fire Power' (*Nandina domestica* 'Fire Power') that huddles in my front bed. It has never popped up over a foot in height, nor does it color sufficiently in fall to be worthwhile, and about eight months of the year it carries hideous brown leaves that refuse to fall off. A spade should be in its future if I had a lick of sense. I chose to move it instead to an area with more sun to see if it would thrive better in the new spot. Likewise, *Clematis integrifolia caerulea* 'Bushy Blue Bell' sprawls everywhere if it isn't staked and besides it's undistinguishable from other *C. integrifolia* cultivars; *Paeonia* 'Primavera' is not anywhere near yellow but only flowers a pale white and should have been eliminated for false advertising; and there is a sprawling stiff stemmed ground cover on the back left of the house (I've forgotten it's name) that spreads and has small yellow flowers for only a week in the spring and just needs to go away.

But why can't I and other gardeners more frequently make the right choice and just assign these misbegotten creatures to the scrap (the compost) heap? Why can't we put them beside the dog bowl and forget about them? Even the great Christopher Lloyd, in *In My Garden* gives the advice, "Thou shalt not kill, but need not strive, officiously to keep alive." For my part, partially it is that I find there is quite enough death in my garden due to my own inadequacies as a gardener to add to the compost pile those who are tough enough to live but who may not be physically appealing. A eugenicist I am decidedly not. No, I prefer instead to neglect the disliked plant until it dies on its own merits, a cruel and unusual punishment for not making the grade, or I move it around to other spots until it finally sulks and is done in by an early freeze or inadvertent prairie fire. Once in a great while, the plant comes around on its own or it likes its new home better and surprises me by seeming worthwhile to grow.

I fully admit my approach to gardening is similar to my approach to parenting. No matter how awkward or unruly the child, I have full faith that time will eventually tease out the best intrinsic qualities of the creature, leaving only satisfaction that our patience has been rewarded at last. The dog bowl shelf is not for unpleasant plants from my garden, any more than it is for wayward teenagers. Well, sometimes it's tempting for teenagers.

About The Author

Dr. James K. Roush is a 2007 Riley County Master Gardener. He now gardens on a shallow façade of clay overlying the chert and limestone bedrock of the Kansas Flint Hills that provides a sharp contrast in gardening experience to the deep Indiana soils he was raised on. When he's not gardening, reading about gardening, or writing about gardening, he is a small animal veterinary orthopedic surgeon and a Professor at the Kansas State University College of Veterinary Medicine. A long-suffering wife and two children share his time and tribulations with the garden.

Index of mentioned plants